How to Calculate Statistics

Carol Taylor Fitz-Gibbon
Lynn Lyons Morris

Center for the Study of Evaluation
University of California, Los Angeles

SAGE PUBLICATIONS Beverly Hills/London

The *Program Evaluation Kit* was developed at the Center for the Study of Evaluation, University of California, Los Angeles. Copyright of this edition is claimed until December 31, 1988. Thereafter all portions of this work covered by this copyright will be in the public domain.

The *Program Evaluation Kit* was developed under a contract with a National Institute of Education, Department of Health, Education and Welfare. However, the opinions expressed herein do not necessarily reflect the position or policy of that agency, and no official endorsement should be inferred.

The *Program Evaluation Kit* is published and distributed by Sage Publications, Inc., Beverly Hills, California under an exclusive agreement with The Regents of the University of California.

For information address:

Sage Publications, Inc.
275 South Beverly Drive
Beverly Hills, California 90212

Sage Publications Ltd
28 Banner Street
London EC1Y 8QE

Printed in the United States of America

International Standard Book Number 0-8039-1072-X
Library of Congress Catalog Card No. 78-58659

SEVENTH PRINTING

Table of Contents

List of Worksheets

Acknowledgements

This book is part of the *Program Evaluation Kit*. The kit contains eight books, each covering a topic commonly confronted by evaluators of educational programs. The kit was developed over a three year period as a project of the Center for the Study of Evaluation (CSE), University of California, Los Angeles, funded by the National Institute of Education. Many people besides the kit's authors contributed to its eventual publication either conceptually or through technical support.

The idea of writing such a kit we owe to Marvin C. Alkin, Director of CSE from 1968 to 1975. Eva L. Baker, current Center Director, provided the continuing solid support and lively interest necessary for its completion. Adrianne Bank, first as co-director of the kit project in its early stages and finally in her role as the Center's Associate Director, gave us the moral support necessary to traverse the arduous stages of kit production.

Several staff members aided in the kit's extensive field test—151 sites throughout the United States and Canada. We thank Margeret Dotseth, Marlene Henerson, Richards Smith Williams, and Esther Goldstein for their painstaking work in gathering and organizing field test data.

The kit books were extensively reviewed by experts in the areas of evaluation research, methodology, and measurement. Comments on the content of this book were made by Ward Keesling, Systems Development Corporation; Leonard Klibanoff, Research Management Corporation; and Leigh Burstein, Shelley Niwa, Jennie Yeh, and Rand Wilcox, all of CSE. These reviewers not only made valuable suggestions for revision of early drafts, but they gave the authors a strong sense of the kit's usefulness as both a procedural guide and educational tool.

The authors wish to thank members of the Center's technical support staff who worked hard to keep manageable the production of such a large work. Donna Anderson Cuvelier carried the major responsibility for typing, organizing, and supervising manuscript preparation. Ruth Paysen ably shouldered part of the burden of typing the extensive manuscript. Proofreading and indexing were handled by Michael Bastone and Mark Young with speed, accuracy, and good humor.

Gracious thanks are also in order to Lou Orsan of Visual Sense, Inc., who provided advice about graphic design in the preparation of the field test draft of the kit and who designed the books finally published.

We are grateful to the Literary Executor of the late Sir Ronald A. Fisher, F.R.S., to Dr. Frank Yates, F.R.S. and to Longman Group Ltd., London, for permission to reprint Table III from their book *Statistical Tables for Biological, Agricultural and Medical Research* (6th edition, 1974).

We wish finally to thank Cheryl Tyler of the UCLA Office of Contracts and Grants who ably ushered the kit through final legal channels toward publication.

Carol Taylor Fitz-Gibbon
Lynn Lyons Morris

Los Angeles, California
August 1978

Chapter 1

An Introduction to the Statistics Included in This Book

The Uses of Statistics

A glance at your dictionary will show you that statistics is an area of mathematics seeking to make order out of collections of diverse facts or data. This is another way of saying that statistics helps you to crunch large amounts of information into usable numbers. A major reason for the development and regular use of statistics is a need to cope with the limited capacity of human working memory. Any human being, asked to think about large quantities of information all at once, quickly loses track. Summarization and abbreviation are always necessary.

Another ongoing objective of statistics is to find those numbers which *most accurately* communicate the nature of attitudes, achievements, and events which need to be described. Statistics aims to condense opinions, performances, and comparisons among them into summary numbers that can be understood in a single glance—or maybe two. These numbers can then be talked about, remembered, and used as bases for making decisions, forming opinions, or developing theories.

Of course, *using* statistics[1] demands knowing what they mean and appreciating their limitations. The objective of this book is to guide you in using statistical methods to summarize the data you collect and report, and to give you some brief instruction about their purpose and interpretation.

Statistics in education has three main purposes. Most evaluations will give you a chance to pursue all three:

1. *Statistics summarize information.* There are two types of summary statistics—measures of central tendency and measures of variability. Means, medians, and modes, called *measures of central tendency,* help you to portray in a single number the central message of a group of numerical scores. *Measures of variability,* such as the standard deviation, qualify measures of central tendency by showing how varied are the scores which contributed to the central tendency number. The smaller the variation, the more representative the mean or median. A *standard deviation* is best thought of as a measure of the average amount that scores vary from their *mean.* A large standard deviation tells you that the mean which it accompanies is *not* to be considered a good summary number for the whole group of scores.

2. *Statistics tell you how seriously to regard apparent differences observed between results of programs or treatments.* If you plan to report that a change occurred in, say, achievement scores or answers to attitude questions, you want to be sure that the change you have uncovered is a real one, not one attributable to the fluctuations that scores naturally undergo. Statistics help you to determine whether or not the result produced by your study or program evaluation is likely to have occurred just by chance. A statistical test takes you through an exercise in which you first assume that the program or treatment you are examining in fact produced *no* effect whatsoever. Showing that in this situation your result would be *highly unusual* supports a case that the *no effect* assumption must be wrong. For example, starting from the *no effect* working assumption, if your study yields a result that could have occurred, say, 75% of the time just by chance, then neither you nor your evaluation's audience will allow the results to influence decisions that are to be made. On the other hand, if you obtain a result of such great magnitude that it could have occurred by chance in the *no effect* situation only rarely—perhaps 5% of the time—then your results will be believable.

3. *Statistics help you determine the amount of relationship among sets of data.* Amount of relationship is usually discovered by means of a correlation. Correlation tells you the degree to which two sets of scores vary together. You might want to know, for instance, whether students' math achievement scores at the end of a year have anything to do with their attitude toward school as expressed by a questionnaire. By correlating these two sets of data, you may come to one of three conclusions:

   a. There is a high positive correlation between the two. This means that the statistic you have calculated has given you a high decimal, less than 1, showing that as scores on one measure—the math achievement test—became higher, the other measure's scores increased as well.

   b. No relationship has been found between the two. This means that your correlation coefficient has yielded a decimal not significantly different from zero.

   c. There is a high negative correlation between the two measures. Your correlation coefficient is a negative decimal close to −1 showing that as scores became higher on

---

1. The word is both singular and plural.

the achievement measure, attitude toward school actually became worse.

The Book's Contents and Format

Display of central tendency, statistical tests and correlation are the major purposes of statistics, and the sole focus of the statistics you will find in this book. An effort has been made to include here only the most basic and commonly used techniques. The methods outlined in this book are not only suited to answering the most essential questions to be asked during an evaluation,[2] but knowing about them will provide you with a strong basis for understanding statistics in general. If you have a chance in the course of your experience as an evaluator, you might want to acquaint yourself with more complicated or more recently developed statistics for special circumstances.

The contents of this book are based on the experience of evaluators at the Center for the Study of Evaluation, University of California, Los Angeles, on advice from experts in the field of educational measurement and statistics, and on the comments of people in school settings who used a field test edition. Though the formulas for computing statistics are fixed, an effort has been made to use the most intuitively understandable computational methods, and to prescribe procedures which help you, whenever possible, to understand how information is manipulated by a statistical procedure to yield a certain sort of result.

How to Calculate Statistics is a workbook; its three main sections (Chapters 2, 3, and 4) are organized around *worksheets.* Each worksheet provides step-by-step instructions for calculating and interpreting one particular statistic. Preceding each worksheet is an *introduction to the worksheet* which explains what the statistic does and when to use it.

The book is divided into five chapters. Chapter 2 deals with measures of central tendency and variability, procedures for *summarizing* a single set of scores. You will use these procedures most often—any time you have a set of scores available to be analyzed and reported. Chapter 3 describes statistics that make *comparisons* between results from two groups, such as the mean achievement test scores from an experimental group and a control group. The statistics in Chapter 3 are usually referred to as *tests of significance* since they help determine how seriously you should regard apparent differences found among the achievements, abilities, or attitudes of groups. In addition to worksheets for performing statistical tests, Chapter 3 contains a section called "What a Test of Statistical Significance Does."

Chapter 4 deals with relationships and *correlations.* This section will be used most often when you want to know if the scores that a group received on one measure are systematically related to the scores the same group received on another measure. For example, you might want to know if children's math scores were related to the number of times

per week those children attended a special math program.

Chapter 5 explains how to prepare data for computer analysis using as an example the most frequently used ready-made set of programs, the *Statistical Package for the Social Sciences (SPSS).*[3] The chapter also describes the relationship between the canned programs available in SPSS and the statistics explained in this book. It contains, as well, a brief description of additional statistical procedures that you can use for data analysis if you have access to a computer.

How you use the worksheets that comprise Chapters 2 through 4 is of course up to you. Most of them can be worked within the book. Others, however, should probably have been called *guidesheets,* since you will have to copy tables or graphs onto your own paper rather than use the worksheet itself. Space simply does not permit this book to provide room for listing large quantities of data.

The worksheets, you will notice, are divided vertically in two, with the *step-by-step instructions* down the left-hand side of each page, and a parallel *worked example* on the right. Please note that these worked examples are fictitious, provided for purposes of illustration. Because they serve this function, examples often present idealized data from situations that have come off without a hitch. Do not be dismayed if your result looks different from the one obtained by the fortunate, but fictitious, evaluator in the example. What is important is that the result you obtain make sense in terms of the numbers it is possible to compute from the procedure provided. If you have selected the proper statistic in the first place, and if you have double-checked your calculations, then an initially funny-looking result is probably correct. If you have doubts, of course, have a data analyst check your work.

The worksheets in Chapters 2, 3, and 4 assume that you have an electronic calculator, most conveniently one with a square root key. In order to be useful to people whose math instruction may have ended years ago, the worksheets demand only minimal math knowledge; and since people often have trouble fitting numbers into formulas, calculations are broken into substeps. Depending on your math experience, of course, you will be able to skip substeps that you find unnecessary.

Chapter 5, by the way, assumes no prior experience with computers.

Using the Book

You have come to this book because you need or want to know more about statistics. If you are reading it solely for professional growth, look thoughtfully through bits of it frequently rather than trying to digest it all at once. As you read about the different analysis methods, try to think of situations within the realm of your own work to which they could be applied. If possible, *use* the procedures with whatever data you have available. Thinking about concrete situations will make the procedures discussed here more

---

2. Another excellent and easy-to-read text that discusses the uses of statistics for particular evaluation tasks is Talmage, H. *Statistics as a tool for educational practitioners.* Berkeley, CA: McCutchan Publishing Corporation, 1976.

3. Nie, N. H., Hull, C. H., Jenkins, J. G., Steinbrenner, K., & Bent, D. H. *Statistical package for the social sciences (2nd ed.).* New York: McGraw-Hill, 1975.

familiar to you so that soon you will be able to quickly select and apply these statistics. What is more, mastering the basic techniques in this book will prepare you to learn about more complex ones.

If you are searching for a statistic *to use right now,* then your first jobs are to organize the data in preparation for statistical analyses and to assure that you locate and perform the right ones. Reading the next section should help you.

Carrying Out Statistical Analyses

Assume that your evaluation or experimental study has come to the point where instruments have been designed, produced or purchased, and administered. Data analysis begins the minute the completed instruments have been returned to you. If some or all of your analysis will be done by computer, read Chapter 5 at this time. If you will need to perform analysis by hand, then Chapter 2 will almost always be your first guide. You will need to produce an easily comprehended and accurate summary of your results. Generally this summary should take two forms:

- One or more graphs
- One or more summary statistics

Graphs and Summary Statistics

To produce a *graph,* first prepare a *data summary sheet.* This is a single sheet of paper on which scores from the instruments are recorded so that they will be easily accessible when you perform computations. If all of your analysis will be done by computer, data can be summarized using a standard coding sheet for the keypunch operator, or they can be punched directly onto tape or cards from the instruments themselves.

Once scores have been organized in one place, use Worksheets 2A or 2B to help you construct a rough graph. The purpose of this graph is not so much to provide a data summary for your report as to give you a chance to *eyeball the data*—to look for trends which will give you hunches about what analyses to perform.

Calculating *summary statistics* will also demand that you first prepare a *data summary sheet.* You might then choose either to compute a mean (an average score) or locate a median (the middle score). The *median,* described on page 18, can be quickly found from a graph or from a rank-ordered list of scores. A rank-ordered list is a set of scores arranged in order from high to low. Along with the median, you should report the upper and lower quartiles, pages 18 and 19, to show the spread or variation in the scores. This gives the reader an idea of the median's representativeness.

The *mean,* Worksheets 2C or 2D, takes longer to calculate, but it is usually preferred since it is often needed for statistical tests. Report the standard deviation, Worksheet 2E, along with the mean to show the spread of scores.

What you do after computing summary statistics depends on the purpose behind your data collection:

1. If conclusions to be drawn from your study depend on having detected a *difference* in the attitudes or achievements of various groups, then you can use statistics to provide the audience with at least part of a basis for judging the importance of the difference you do find. Usually this means computing a test of *statistical significance*; but another statistical examination of differences, calculation of *confidence limits,* is possible—and recommended—as well.

2. If you wish to detect whether various characteristics of students or programs are related to each other, then you can use correlational methods to estimate the strength of these relationships.

Statistics for Examining Differences

If a *design* has been used to assign groups to experimental and control treatments, your study has a built-in basis for determining what gains the experimental program or procedure brought about: the control group tells you what results you would have obtained *without* the program. You can answer the critical question, *Has the program made a difference?* by examining divergences in the posttest results you have obtained from the experimental and control groups. Statistics focusing on an obtained difference tell you whether it is large enough to support the conclusion that a *real* difference exists between the groups.

You might use statistics in conjunction with a design to scrutinize differences in group performance at the *beginning* as well as at the end of a program. Attention to differences in attitudes or achievement at the beginning of a program or experiment helps you to establish a case for the *initial equality* of experimental and control groups—a critical exercise if you hope to interpret differences at the study's conclusion.

In the *absence* of design and under certain restricted conditions, you might, as well, use a statistical test to examine the size of the difference between pretest and posttest scores produced by a *single* group. Or you might want to determine whether two groups of people, say boys and girls, perform differently on some measure.

If you wish to compare scores—either those obtained by *two* groups on a single measure or by one group at *two* different times—you will want to compute either a *test of significance* or a set of *confidence limits.*

You might, in some circumstances, find that you need to compare results from *more than two* groups. This would be the case, for example, if you were conducting an evaluation which compared two experimental programs with a control group. When you must compare results from more than two groups, you will need to use *analysis of variance* (ANOVA) described briefly on page 138. Most analyses of variance are too complicated to be computed by hand, even with the aid of a calculator, so worksheets for ANOVA are not included in this book. Should you decide that an ANOVA is appropriate to your situation, then find a data analyst to perform the analysis for you by computer. Your local education district office or a graduate student in education or psychology at a local university can quickly set up an ANOVA.

Tests of statistical significance

Most often researchers base judgments about whether or not an observed difference is an important one on tests of statistical significance. While quite a few different tests can be used, depending on different characteristics of the data, all tests of statistical significance follow a common procedure:

1. Through a combination of statistical theory and computation, they construct a table or graph showing the probability of obtaining various-sized *observed* score differences in the situation where *no actual difference* exists between groups.

2. They compare *your* observed difference with this table to determine whether it is *rare enough* to allow you to conclude that your finding probably does represent a *true* difference.

The introduction to Chapter 3, pages 35 to 38 , presents the logical bases of statistical tests in greater detail, as well as a discussion of what statistical significance means to the evaluator.

Confidence limits

While a test of significance tells you whether the difference you have found between scores is big enough to transcend chance, *confidence limits give you an estimate of the differences you would obtain between the experimental and control groups were you to repeat the study again and again.* In this way confidence limits provide more information for the user than do tests of significance. They not only show *that* a true difference has probably been found; they also provide an idea of the *size* of the difference.

What is more, computing confidence limits still permits a test of statistical significance. Since confidence limits use the difference you have obtained to describe the range of differences you *might have* found between group scores, a statistically significant obtained difference will be one whose confidence limits *exclude* a difference of zero. This reasoning is put forward more fully in Chapter 3, which instructs you in computing confidence limits and tests of statistical significance in nearly any situation when the performances or attitudes of two groups are to be compared. If you have appropriate data and if your audience can be educated to the point of preferring and using confidence limits, then by all means use them.

Statistics for Detecting Relationships: Correlations

Perhaps in addition to or instead of a concern about whether your study has produced differences in group performance, you want to know whether relationships exist among student, teacher, and/or program characteristics. In this case, you are interested in calculating a correlation. Correlations are especially useful for answering these common questions:

- Is there a relationship between student, teacher, or school scores on *two measures* which have been administered?

- What is the strength of the relationship between *a measure* which has been administered and a certain *characteristic* of the students, teachers, or schools such as their socio-economic status?

In addition, you might have more specialized reasons for computing a correlation. These following questions reflect the concerns of people who develop measurement instruments such as achievement tests, attitude surveys, and observation schedules:

- What is the *reliability* of a test or an attitude instrument?

- What is the instrument's predictive or concurrent *validity*?

- How *reliable* are the reports of two observers?

If you plan to calculate correlation coefficients, turn to Chapter 4. You will notice that confidence limits and tests of significance can be computed for correlations to allow you to decide how much faith to place in them.

Some Terminology

Work with statistics demands precision, not only in collection and computation of numbers, but in vocabulary. The book's procedures talk again and again about scores, instruments, cases, and groups. Each of these terms is a catch-all word used in place of a whole list or phrase so that discussions do not become overly complicated.

Scores and data. Data consist most basically of *scores*. In general, scores are numbers that represent the performance of students on a test. Sometimes, however, the data you will analyze will not consist of scores in this usual sense. The data, for instance, may be made up of *observations* of the percentage of times a child attends to his work; or the data may consist of *ratings* provided by teachers, or a *count* of the number of parents at a meeting, or *ranks* showing students' classroom positions. Rather than constantly referring by name to the many forms that pieces of information might take, this book simply uses the word *scores*. Please, then, interpret *score* quite broadly to mean *any number produced by a measuring instrument.* Use the term *datum* to mean the same thing, with the plural *data* referring to a collection of scores.

Instrument, measuring instrument, or measure. These terms refer to *any means by which information is obtained.* The following are all considered measurement instruments: purchased or locally made achievement tests, observations, interviews, records, reports, checklists, and questionnaires.

Cases. Often the evaluator uses statistics with scores from individual people—parents, teachers, principals, or students. Sometimes, however, the evaluator might need to apply statistical tests to single scores from classrooms, schools, or districts. If, for instance, classrooms have been randomly assigned to one program or another, then data may be collected in the form of classroom averages.[4] In this situation, the cases or units whose scores go into the statistical formula will be *classrooms*. In general, the term *case* will mean *whatever single person or collection of persons provides each score.* Thus cases might be students, members of a particular student classification, classrooms, teachers, parents, schools, districts, and so forth.

Group. The term group in this book refers to treatment groups. A treatment group is a set of cases—students, districts, whatever—*who are all receiving the same program* or experimental treatment. Tests of statistical significance assume that an experimental group is receiving the program being evaluated or pilot tested, and some control group is receiving either a competing program, the old program, or no program at all.

---

4. Whether your study focuses on scores of individuals, classrooms, or schools will depend on the *unit of analysis* you have chosen. This choice will be determined by statements which you intend to make based on your results. If recommendations will be made about classroom practices, then your unit of analysis will be the classroom; and the scores which you collect and summarize will be classroom averages. Similarly, if you wish to make statements about the treatment of certain students, then the unit will be the student and you will report mean scores or percent of students producing certain scores per focus group. Discussions of unit of analysis are contained in most experimental or evaluation design texts. See, in particular: Fitz-Gibbon, C. T., & Morris, L. L. How to design a program evaluation. In L. L. Morris (Ed.), *Program evaluation kit*. Beverly Hills: Sage Publications, 1978.

Chapter 2

Summarizing a Set of Scores From the Administration of a Measure to One Group

If you have ever tried it, you know how difficult it is to read down a long list of scores and get a firm grasp on what the scores are telling you: *What is their range? What score represents the average? Are there more high or more low scores?* The first step in data analysis, therefore, is data reduction. This is accomplished through methods that display the data in the form of a graph, or that reduce the data to a few numbers which *summarize* the whole set of scores. The following worksheets describe procedures for data reduction:

Introduction to Worksheets 2A and 2B
Graphing a Distribution of Scores

This procedure produces a *graph* showing how many times each score has occurred, that is, displaying the *frequency* of each score. The graph illustrates what is called the *distribution* of scores.

First, a horizontal *axis*, or line, is drawn on graph paper, allowing each square to represent a score value or values. The score for each case, represented by an X, is then placed on this axis. X's pile up in a vertical column when several cases get the same score or have scores in the same category. A vertical axis may then be drawn, and numbers added to denote the frequency of each score.

Example. A set of scores plotted on a graph:

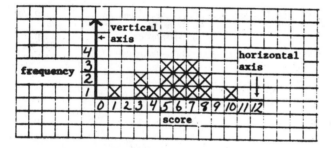

Here, the same scores have been *grouped* into score categories:

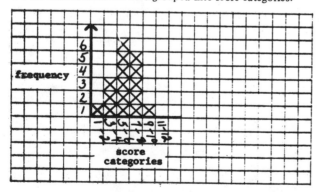

When To Graph Scores

Scores collected from achievement, implementation, and attitude information should be graphed whenever your situation matches one of the following:

1. *You need to see how the set of scores looks in order to describe it.* Are most of the scores clustered at one end? Or evenly spread? Do the scores seem to form a *normal distribution*—that is, are there a few high and low scores and many average scores making for a *hump-in-the-middle* appearance ⌒ ?

2. *You want to check for outliers.* Outliers are extremely high or low scores. When plotted, such scores appear isolated from the main group of scores. Sometimes an outlier represents an unusual occurrence and should be removed from the data. For example, you might ask a teacher about a student's score which was practically zero and discover that the child had been summoned to the office right after the test started. Or suppose you had a list of gain scores (posttest minus pretest for each student) with one score showing an enormous gain. Checking pretest papers, you might find that the student's pretest score had been incorrectly recorded as 05 instead of 50. In general, when you see an outlier, you should ask: *Is this a score from a very unusual case or was there some error in the administration of the measure, the recording of the data, or in computations which may have been performed to yield the score?* If the score seems likely to be the result of an error, discard it.

   Even if the score *is* valid, you may want to discard it if its inclusion would unreasonably affect the results. For example, if a control group happened to contain a phenomenally bright child whose unusually high scores pull up the group's mean, it might be a good idea *not* to include the child's scores in your analysis. Of course, you should mention this decision, complete with rationale, in your report.

3. *You need to locate the median score and other quartiles.* A set of scores is well described by stating the *median* and the *upper and lower* (sometimes called the first and fourth) *quartiles.* These can be easily found by counting off scores from one end of a plotted distribution. The median is the middle score or 50th percentile point of a distribution: 50% of the scores are above the median, 50% below it. The lower quartile is the point below which lies one quarter (25%) of the scores. The upper quartile represents the point below which three quarters (75%) of the scores have fallen.

Example. Fifty-seven scores are plotted on a graph, as indicated by the postscript *n=57*.

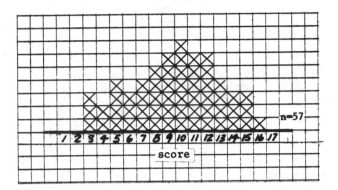

Because half of 57 is 28.5, the median, rounding up, will be the 29th score. Counting from the left or right up and down each column locates the 29th score. The number along the horizontal axis corresponding to this score, 10, is the median.

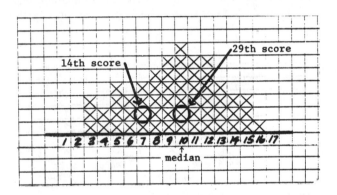

Since $57 \div 4 = 14.25$, the lower quartile, below which 1/4 of the scores lie, will appear between the 14th and 15th scores. Since these scores are both 7, the 25th percentile, or lower quartile, is 7.

4. *You intend to use the set of scores for assigning students to programs or for dividing them into subgroups.* You may need, for instance, to assign a school's lowest achievers to a compensatory program. Or, if you are selecting a random sample of a district's schools, you might want to first divide them into groups with histories of high, average, and low achievement. Assuring that you sample a proportionate number from each stratum strengthens your claim that the sample is representative of the whole district. In either of these situations, you will need to select *cutoff scores*—scores which form the boundaries among the groups you intend to define. The cutoff for selecting students will be a score on a particular achievement or aptitude test; for schools it will be the average school score on such a measure. Graphing is a good preliminary to choosing cutoff scores. The graph is a picture of how scores tend to group themselves.

Interpreting Graphs

This section describes a few kinds of distributions you might produce using Worksheets 2A or 2B.

Possibility 1: There are a lot of average scores with a few high and low scores on each side

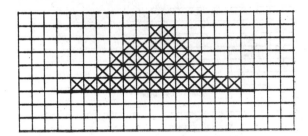

A distribution that looks like the figure will occur often and can be roughly described as a *normal distribution.*[5] Such an array of scores is also *unimodal.* The *mode* is the most usual score; *uni*modal distributions have just one peak.

If there are few extreme scores, the distribution may be *steeply peaked:*

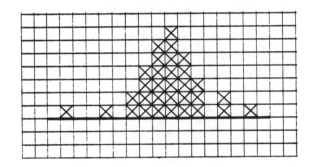

Or, if there are a large number of high and low scores, you might find a *flattened* distribution:

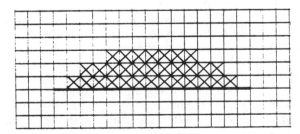

All three of these distributions can be considered *unimodal* and *symmetric.* They will correspond roughly, for most purposes, to a normal distribution.

---

5. The normal distribution is mathematically defined. A distribution which is close to normal will have certain standard properties which make possible various statistical statements.

Possibility 2: Scores are mainly high or mainly low

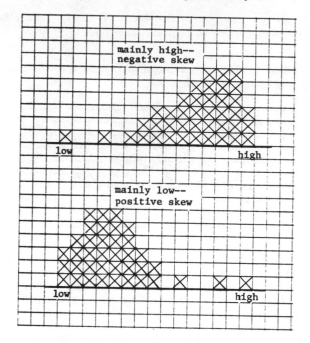

These are called *skewed* distributions. The distribution with mainly high scores is called a *negatively skewed* distribution; the one with mainly low scores is a *positively skewed* distribution.[6]

A negatively skewed distribution could indicate that the measure producing the scores has a *ceiling*.

It does not give potentially high scorers a chance to score *high enough* to produce a more normal distribution. You should suspect that an achievement test is showing a ceiling effect, for example, when the brightest students all score about the same. The ceiling is probably a result of the absence of enough difficult items to allow the brightest students to show their strength. However, if the test has been designed to measure *mastery* of certain skills and you expect most students to achieve mastery, then a negatively skewed distribution is what you will want to see.

A test producing negatively skewed distributions might be useful to you in another way. Since scores at the lower end of such a test are well spread out, the test might be a useful one for selecting students to take part in a remedial program. Notice that the pile of scores at the *top* makes the test *unsuitable* for selection at that end of the scale.

---

6. A way to remember this non-intuitive distinction is to use imagery. Think of the large collection of scores at either end as the body of an animal. The correct skewedness label for the distribution corresponds to where the animal rests its tail—at the high end for positively skewed distributions, and at the low end for those with negative skew.

A positively skewed distribution occurs when there are many more low scores on the test than high scores.

This could indicate a *floor* to the test: the easy items are so easy that almost all students answer them correctly, but only a few students can answer the more difficult questions. It is as though the normal curve were pushed in at the lower end, eliminating very low scores because of several easy items. People who could have scored even *lower* were not given a chance. If the low scores are all *very* low, this could indicate that almost all the items are difficult. A test of this sort would be useful for selecting students for gifted or accelerated programs because scores at the high end of the scale are well spread out.

Notice that skewedness does not only apply to distributions of scores from ability and achievement tests. A skewed distribution can be produced by an attitude scale when almost everyone gives either positive or negative responses:

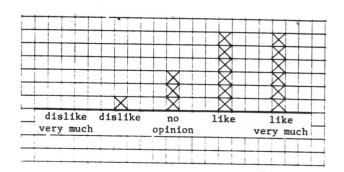

Possibility 3: Scores pile up at two different parts of the scale

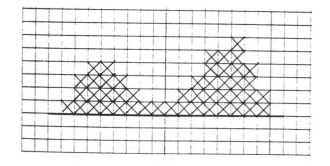

This is called a *bimodal* distribution. If an *achievement* test yields such a distribution, investigate further:

• The test might have a *breakthrough* built into it—students who can answer some items can answer a whole set of other items; students who cannot are stumped.

- The students may represent two levels of development or experience. For instance, were you to graph results on a spelling test for a group composed of equal numbers of third graders and fifth graders, it would not be surprising if you found two humps in your graph, one mostly from the scores of third graders and the other from the scores of fifth graders. In most situations, however, it will remain for you to *discover* the characteristics or differences in experience that best explain the gap between the two achievement levels.

Bimodal score distributions from *attitude* measures indicate that respondents are falling into groups with different opinions. If the two modal opinions—the two peaks—are on opposite sides of the neutral point, as in the graph, the bimodal distribution indicates *polarization.*

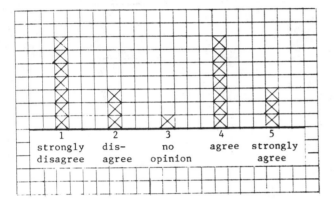

If you should find that your scores yield a bimodal (or perhaps *multimodal*) distribution, you will have to use great care when discussing and summarizing them. For one thing, *when a distribution is clearly bimodal, it cannot be described by reporting a single statistic, such as the median or the mean score.* In the graph above, the mean score is about 3—"no opinion"—but reporting this mean would not at all convey the way the group responded to the attitude question. If a distribution is bimodal, this should be reported and both modes should be noted.

Possibility 4: Scores occur about equally often all along the scale

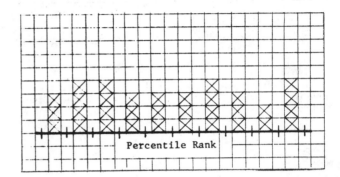

This is called a *rectangular distribution.* It is the distribution you would get if you plotted the percentile scores in a school district that contained the same number of students at each achievement level all the way from barely-achieving-at-all to superior. The rectangular distribution is rare, and it presents no particular interpretation problems. You have simply gotten about equal results across the board.

Worksheet 2A
Graphing a Distribution of Scores by Hand

Steps	Example

Step 1. Prepare a data summary sheet

Make a list of the cases (students, classes, etc.) and the scores you intend to graph for each. Find yourself some graph paper.

Step 1. Prepare a data summary sheet

In this case, a list is made of 26 students and their achievement test scores.

Results on a 20-item test

Student	Score
Arlene Apple	13
Brian Berry	8
Carol Cooper	13
David Dear	10
Evan Evans	7
Fred Fink	10
Graham Garden	9
Helen Handler	15
Ivan Inglis	13
John Jones	6
Kevin Kendall	6
Linda Lee	4
Marlene Mann	8
Norbert Norris	14
Odette Orme	7
Penny Parker	11
Quinton Quin	10
Rosa Robinson	12
Saul Sanchez	12
Trevor Taylor	14
Upton Ulm	9
Valerie Venn	11
Wendy Williams	8
Xavier Xerxes	13
Yolanda Young	10
Zelda Zee	12

Step 2. Choose a convenient scale

Decide how many squares you are going to need on the horizontal axis. This will determine the scale of the graph. To do this, you will need to:

a. Decide what range of scores must be shown. Do you want the axis to represent:

· the range of possible scores? This is the range from zero to the top score possible on the test.

· the range of obtained scores? This is the range from the highest score on the list to the lowest score on the list.

Step 2. Choose a convenient scale

The achievement test had 20 items, so a 20-square axis is necessary. This is the range of possible scores. The range of obtained scores was 12: from 4, the lowest score, to 15, the highest score.

Steps	Example

b. Then decide whether each square on the axis will represent a <u>single</u> score or a score <u>category</u>. Examples of these two types of horizontal scale were shown on page 18.

<u>Step 3. Prepare the horizontal axis</u>

Draw the horizontal axis, and label a convenient number of boxes.

<u>Step 4. Plot scores on the graph</u>

Read a score from the data summary sheet, and mark an X in the box for that score value on the horizontal axis. Repeat for all scores in the list, piling the X's into a vertical column when several scores are the same.

<u>Step 5. Label the graph</u>

Add a <u>key</u>, and label the axes and the graph.

<u>Step 3. Prepare the horizontal axis</u>

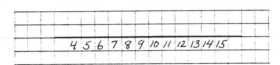

<u>Step 4. Plot scores on the graph</u>

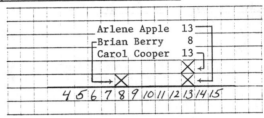

You will not, of course, write in the student's name.

<u>Step 5. Label the graph</u>

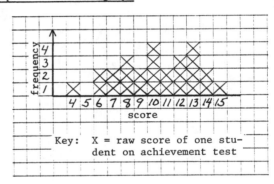

PREVIEW TO AN ALTERNATIVE METHOD

Worksheet 2B, on the following pages, describes a way to display and graph a set of scores right in your typewriter.

Graphing a Distribution
of Scores by Typewriter

Steps	Example

Step 1. Prepare a data summary sheet

Step 1. Prepare a data summary sheet

A list is made of 26 students and their achievement test scores.

Results on a 20-item test

Student	Score
Arlene Apple	13
Brian Berry	8
Carol Cooper	13
David Dear	10
Evan Evans	7
Fred Fink	10
Graham Garden	9
Helen Handler	15
Ivan Inglis	13
John Jones	6
Kevin Kendall	6
Linda Lee	4
Marlene Mann	8
Norbert Norris	14
Odette Orme	7
Penny Parker	11
Quinton Quin	10
Rosa Robinson	12
Saul Sanchez	12
Trevor Taylor	14
Upton Ulm	9
Valerie Venn	11
Wendy Williams	8
Xavier Xerxes	13
Yolanda Young	10
Zelda Zee	12

Step 2. Convert the data summary sheet into a score-frequency list

To do this, list the scores in a column from high to low. Include all possible scores between the highest and lowest even if no one actually obtained the score. You may want to use score categories rather than individual scores if the range is very large. After listing the scores.

Step 2. Convert the data summary sheet into a score-frequency list

from high to low, refer to the data summary sheet and tally the scores as in column 2 of the example. Then list the frequencies (column 3) by counting the tallies.

1 Score	2 Tally	3 Frequency	4 Graph
20		0	
19		0	
18		0	
17		0	
16		0	
15	/	1	
14	//	2	
13	////	4	
12	///	3	
11	//	2	
10	////	4	
9	//	2	
8	///	3	
7	//	2	
6	//	2	
5		0	
4	/	1	
3		0	
2		0	
1		0	

Step 3. Plot the scores

On the row for each score, type X's to represent the frequency of the score. This could be done directly on the score-frequency list or on a freshly prepared list of scores which omits columns 2 and 3.

Consider this option: Instead of using X's, type the character B for a boy's score and G for a girl's score. The resulting graph could alert you to differences between results from boys and girls.

Step 3. Plot the scores

1 Score	2 Tally	3 Frequency	4 Graph
20		0	
19		0	
18		0	
17		0	
16		0	
15	/	1	X
14	//	2	XX
13	////	4	XXXX
12	///	3	XXX
11	//	2	XX
10	////	4	XXXX
9	//	2	XX
8	///	3	XXX
7	//	2	XX
6	//	2	XX
5		0	
4	/	1	X
3		0	
2		0	
1		0	

Introduction to Worksheets 2C and 2D
Calculating the Mean, $\bar{x}$

The mean of a set of scores is the average score. It is represented by the symbol $\bar{x}$, read as *x bar*.

$$\text{Mean} = \frac{\text{sum of scores}}{\text{number of scores}} \quad \text{that is,} \quad \text{Mean} = \frac{\text{Sum } x}{n} = \bar{x}$$

The mean score is a balance point. If the scores were weights on a ruler, the mean would be the spot at which the ruler would balance.

Example

Scores

```
        11
         9
         9
         6
         3
         2
Sum x = 40

    n = 6

Mean = 40/6 = 6.67 = x̄
```

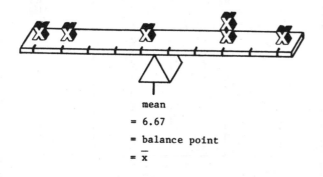

```
mean
= 6.67
= balance point
= x̄
```

When To Use the Mean

Use the mean when you want to and *can* represent a set of scores by using a single numeral. "How can a whole group of scores be well represented by a single number?" you might ask. This depends on the set of scores. If scores are unimodal and tend to cluster fairly close together, then the mean will be a good representative. Otherwise, be wary of reporting only the mean, and make public your doubts of its adequacy. Do *not* use the mean if the distribution of scores is *bimodal,* as discussed on page xx; watch out for this situation with attitude responses particularly. Be careful, in addition, to check for *outliers* before computing the mean. Since the mean is a balance point, it can be heavily influenced by extremes if you have only a small number of scores.

The mean is an extensively used and useful indicator of group performance. Evaluations often focus major interest on *mean* scores from groups of students or classrooms since large-scale programs generally aim at improving the general achievement or attitude level of groups receiving various programs rather than concentrating on the performance of individual students.

If you want to describe a set of scores via a single number, however, there is an alternative to using the mean. This alternative is the *median* which, as described on page 19, can be located quickly on a graph showing the distribution of the set of scores. *You may want to use the median rather than the mean if:*

- You will *not* need to perform statistical tests which require the mean.

- You need a quickly obtained estimate of group performance.

- There are outliers which you have not had time to examine. Unlike the mean, the median is not influenced by outliers.

Calculating the Mean
Directly From the Data

Steps	Example

Example

Background

Student	Score on test
John	4
Mary	8
Susan	6
May	10
David	2

Steps

Step 1. Compute the sum

Add up all the scores to get the sum of the scores, sum x.

Step 1. Compute the sum

Total = sum x = 30

Step 2. Count the number of scores you just added, and call this number n

Step 2. Count the number of scores you just added, and call this number n

Number of scores = n = 5

Step 3. Divide the sum of the scores (sum x, the result of Step 1), by the number of scores (n, the result of Step 2)

The result is the average score--the mean.

Step 3. Divide the sum of the scores by the number of scores

Mean score = $\frac{30}{5}$ = 6

PREVIEW TO AN ALTERNATIVE METHOD

The above method will always work. There may be shortcuts sometimes, however. On the next page is an example of how to calculate the mean if you start with a list of how many cases received each score. This method might be quicker if you are calculating the mean score of many students, classrooms, or whatever.

Worksheet 2C

Calculating the Mean
Directly From the Data

Worksheet 2D
Calculating the Mean From Score-Frequency Data

Steps	Example

Example

Background

These are the scores:

John	5
Susan	3
Mary	5
David	2
Leroy	4
Cheryl	8
Tony	4
Peter	3
Thomas	5

Steps

Step 1. Start with a score-frequency table

If possible, have results reported to you in terms of the number of cases (students, parents, classrooms, etc.) receiving each score.

Step 1. Start with a score-frequency table

Here is the score-frequency table made from the scores. Teachers were asked to arrange results in this way to save the evaluator time. The number of students column is the frequency.

Score (out of 10)	Number of students who got the score
10	0
9	0
8	1
7	0
6	0
5	3
4	2
3	2
2	1
1	0
0	0

Step 2. Multiply each score by the frequency of that score

Step 2. Multiply each score by the frequency of that score

You would make an extra column for Step 2 and calculate the mean as shown on the next page.

	Steps			Example	

Score (out of 10)	Number of students who got the score	Score times frequency
10	0	10 x 0 = 0
9	0	9 x 0 = 0
8	1	8 x 1 = 8
7	0	etc. 0
6	0	0
5	3	15
4	2	8
3	2	6
2	1	2
1	0	0
0	0	0
	9 (total number of scores)	39 (sum of scores)

Step 3. Add up all the answers from Step 2 to get the sum of all the scores (sum x)

 = sum x

Step 4. Add up all the frequencies to get the total number of scores (n)

[ ] = n

Step 5. Divide the sum of scores by the number of scores to get the mean

[ ] = $\frac{\text{sum x}}{\text{n}}$ = Mean

Step 3. Add up all the answers from Step 2 to get the sum of all the scores (sum x)

Sum of scores = 39

Step 4. Add up all the frequencies to get the total number of scores (n)

Total number of scores = 9

Step 5. Divide the sum of scores by the number of scores to get the mean

Mean = $\frac{39}{9}$ = 4 3/9

= 4 1/3

= 4.33

Introduction to Worksheet 2E
Calculating the Standard Deviation s and Variance s²

The standard deviation of a group of scores is a number which tells you whether most of those scores *cluster closely around their mean* or are *spread out* along the scale. The standard deviation is useful not only for describing distributions but also for comparing groups. Furthermore, it provides the basis for *standardizing* test scores by computing, for instance, stanines, I.Q.'s, and scale scores.

The meaning of the term *standard deviation* can be understood by considering the meaning of the word *deviation. A deviation is the distance of a score from the mean for its group.* If a group of scores has a mean of 10, then the deviation of a score of 15 is 5 points. The deviation of a score of 6 is -4 points. Six is 4 points *below* 10; 15 is 5 points *above* 10. The standard deviation, symbolized simply as *s*, is similar to, but not equivalent to, the average of the deviations of the scores (ignoring the negative signs). The larger the standard deviation, the further away from the mean the scores are, on average. Thus *the standard deviation of a set of scores is a statistic which shows how much the scores are spread out around the mean. The larger the standard deviation, the more spread out are the scores.*

The *variance*, s², is simply the square of the standard deviation, that is, the standard deviation multiplied by itself. It is often used in statistical calculations instead of the standard deviation itself.

Knowing the standard deviation of a group of scores performs two functions for you:

- It gives you a good means for describing the spread of the scores obtained from the administration of a particular instrument.

- It provides a basis for later statistical procedures that you might want to perform, such as tests of the significance of differences between group means. You will notice, if you look ahead in this book, that the standard deviation fits into many of the formulas for performing statistical tests.

When To Use the Standard Deviation

Whenever you report the *mean* of a set of scores, report the standard deviation along with it. However, if you have more than, say, 100 scores to deal with, you may find calculation of the mean and standard deviation too time-consuming. If you do not *have* to report them and do not need them for statistical tests, then you might choose to report instead the median and upper and lower quartiles described on page 18.

Example. A distribution with a *small* standard deviation:

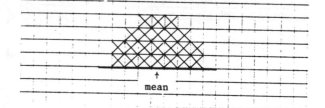

mean

Example: A distribution with a *large* standard deviation:

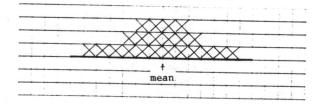

mean

Calculating the Standard Deviation s
and Variance s²

Steps	Example

PREVIEW

The <u>variance</u>, s^2, will be calculated from the formula:

$$s^2 = \frac{\text{sum } (x-c)^2 - nk^2}{n-1}$$

The <u>standard deviation</u>, s, will then be found by taking the square root of the variance. That is,

$$s = \sqrt{s^2}$$

In the variance formula:

x = a score

n = the number of scores

c = the whole-number part of the mean, or average score

k = the fractional part of the mean, or average score

Sum $(x-c)^2$ means that you must use each x value to compute the quantity $(x-c)^2$ and add up all these quantities to get their sum.

Notice that c and k add up to the mean in the variance formula. That is,

$$\bar{x} = c + k$$

Steps	Example

Step 1. List all the scores and find their mean

The mean, $\overline{x}$, is the sum of the scores divided by the number of scores.

Step 1. List all the scores and find their mean

Student	Score	Student	Score
B. Brown	36	C. Orfu	26
R. Brown	23	R. O'Shea	28
C. Bush	34	E. Peck	31
A. Byrne	24	J. Pine	29
S. Cash	35	M. Pinsk	28
N. Chase	24	E. Ruiz	26
J. Chu	25	F. Smith	30
R. Crum	33	R. Smith	27
P. Doud	26	D. Soto	27
W. Duffy	25	J. Souza	30
I. Fiore	33	M. Spitz	28
J. Fink	27	T. Spur	27
P. Good	30	Z. Star	27
D. Gubar	26	P. Stein	26
V. House	32	F. Tuck	16
M. Koch	25	M. Usian	37
G. Lee	31	J. White	29
J. Lieu	32	P. White	29
P. Olson	28	M. Yasuda	31

$$\text{Mean} = \frac{\text{Sum}}{n} = \frac{1081}{38}$$

$$\text{Mean (or } \overline{x}) = 28.447$$

Step 2. Compute the sum of squared deviations

To do this:

First, <u>subtract</u> from each score the whole-number part, c, of the mean. Record the result for each score in a column next to the list of scores. These results are the <u>deviations from c</u>.

Second, <u>multiply</u> each deviation by itself to get the squared deviation for each score.

Third, <u>add</u> up all the squared deviations to get their sum.

Step 2. Compute the sum of squared deviations

In this example, the mean is 28.447, so c—the whole-number part of the mean—is 28. Therefore, the deviation of each score will be its distance from 28. Finding these deviations, squaring them, and finding the sum of the squared deviations produces the following table:

Score x	Deviation x-c	Squared deviation $(x-c)^2$	Score x	Deviation x-c	Squared deviation $(x-c)^2$
36	8	64	26	−2	4
23	−5	25	28	0	0
34	6	36	31	3	9
24	−4	16	29	1	1
35	7	49	28	0	0
24	−4	16	26	−2	4
25	−3	9	30	2	4
33	5	25	27	−1	1
26	−2	4	27	−1	1
25	−3	9	30	2	4
33	5	25	28	0	0
27	−1	1	27	−1	1
30	2	4	27	−1	1
26	−2	4	26	−2	4
32	4	16	16	−12	144
25	−3	9	37	9	81
31	3	9	29	1	1
32	4	16	29	1	1
28	0	0	31	3	9

Steps	Example
Step 3. Subtract the quantity nk^2 from the result of Step 2	**Step 3. Subtract the quantity nk^2 from the result of Step 2**

Step 3. Subtract the quantity nk^2 from the result of Step 2

The fractional part of the mean, k, is squared and then multiplied by n, the number of scores. This product is then subtracted from the result of Step 2.

Notice that if the mean is a whole number, then its fractional part, k, equals zero, and subtracting zero from the result of Step 2 will leave that result unchanged.

Step 4. Compute the variance, s^2

This is accomplished by dividing the result of Step 3 by a number that is one less than the number of scores. In other words, divide by n-1.

Step 5. Compute the standard deviation, s

To get the standard deviation, take the square root of the value you obtained at the end of Step 4.

Step 6. Interpret the statistic

The larger the standard deviation, the more spread out the scores. A small standard deviation will be found when scores all cluster close to the mean.

The standard deviation can be used to describe the performance of a student (or class, or school, etc.) relative to the whole group. By measuring the distance between an individual score and the mean in terms of standard deviations, you can find out whether the score is exceptional or typical. For instance, if s=3, a score of 39 is "3 standard deviations" from a mean of 30--9 points away. Since most scores lie within one standard deviation of the mean, and nearly <u>all</u> the rest lie between one and two, then you know that a score 3 standard deviations away is very rare.

For most distributions that you will encounter, about two-thirds of the members of the group will have a score that is within one standard deviation of the mean. Thus if the mean of a set of scores is 50, and the standard deviation of these scores is 10, about two-thirds of the scores should lie between 40 and 60:

$$\bar{x} = 50 \text{ and } s = 10$$

$$\bar{x} - s = 40$$

$$\bar{x} + s = 60$$

Step 3. Subtract the quantity nk^2 from the result of Step 2

$$k = .447$$

$$k^2 = k \cdot k = .2$$

$$n = 38$$

$$nk^2 = 38(.2) = 7.6$$

Subtracting 7.6 from the result of Step 2 produces:

$$605 - 7.6 = 597.4$$

Step 4. Compute the variance, s^2

$$n - 1 = 38 - 1 = 37$$

$$s^2 = \frac{597.4}{37} = 16.15$$

Step 5. Compute the standard deviation, s

$$s = \sqrt{s^2} = \sqrt{16.15}$$

$$s = 4.02$$

Step 6. Interpret the statistic

These 38 scores have a standard deviation of about 4. A graph can be constructed to show the distance of each score from the mean.

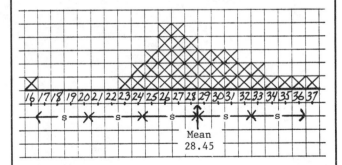

Each **X** represents one student obtaining the score below it. The distance of any score from the mean in terms of standard deviations can be seen on the graph. For example, a score of 36 is almost two standard deviations above the mean.

The lowest score, 16, appears to be quite isolated from all other obtained scores. A score of 16 is lower than 16.39, which is the point that is <u>three standard deviations</u> lower than the mean:

Steps	Example

The standard deviation can also be used to determine if any of the scores are so different from the others that they should be discussed separately or disregarded. As a rule of thumb, if a score is more than 3 standard deviations away from the mean, then you may choose to drop it from your analysis.

$$\overline{x} - 3s = 28.45 - 3\ (4.02)$$
$$= 28.45 - 12.06$$
$$= 16.39$$

Since the score of 16 is lower than three standard deviations below the mean, it can be dropped from the analysis. That is, the mean and standard deviation can be computed as if that student had not been a member of the group.

For the remaining 37 scores, the <u>new mean</u> is:

$$\overline{x} = \frac{1065}{37} = 28.784$$

Since the value of c is still 28, the sum of squared deviations from c can be found by simply subtracting 144, the contribution of the eliminated score to the squared deviation column, from the previous total. So the new sum is:

$$\text{Sum } (x-c)^2 = 605 - 144 = 461$$

The new nk^2 is:

$$nk^2 = 37\ (.784)^2 = 37\ (.6147) = 22.75$$

The new variance, then, is:

$$s^2 = \frac{461 - 22.75}{36} = \frac{438.25}{36} = 12.17$$

Finally, the standard deviation is:

$$s = \sqrt{12.17} = 3.49$$

The new graph is presented below.

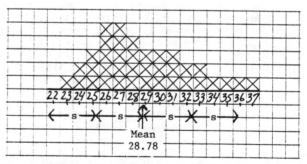

What has changed? The mean has increased about a third of a point, going from 28.45 to 28.78. The standard deviation has gone from about 4 to about 3½.

Chapter 3

Examining the Differences You Have Found Between Scores From Two Groups on the Same Measure

Did your experimental classes produce significantly higher test scores in geometry than the controls?

Can you demonstrate that the phonics program students did better in reading than the look-say program students?

Was there a significant change in attitude toward school between the beginning and the end of the program?

These are the kinds of questions dealt with in this chapter: all involve examining the difference you have obtained between the mean performances of two groups in the interest of finding statistical significance.

Before you conduct tests of statistical significance, you might want to learn a bit about the logical process that a statistical test follows. If you would, then the statistics game presented in the next section should help. If you are eager to get to work, however, then save the game and its subsequent discussion until later, skip to column two of page 38, and find the proper procedure for examining differences between group scores.

What a Test of Statistical Significance Does

You will notice as you examine the worksheets in this chapter that statistical tests have a basic pattern that keeps repeating itself:

1. You calculate a number from your data, and
2. You compare this number with some other number found in a table.

How your computed number measures up to this tabled number tells you whether or not your result is *statistically significant* at some *level*, such as the conventional *.05 or 5%*. To help you better understand what this recurrent

procedure is all about, this section presents a game. If this is your first exposure to these concepts, good understanding will probably require several readings and some careful thought. These are the ideas that have confounded students of statistics for years!

The statistics game

For the purpose of this statistics game, suppose you have a huge quantity of red and white poker chips. You and your *chips accountant* (CPA) are going to conduct a series of trials. Before each trial, the CPA will put 40 chips into a bag which is quaintly called the *population bag*. This will be done out of your sight. Usually she will put in 20 red chips and 20 white chips; but occasionally she will make a change, putting in an unequal number of chips.

To begin with, the only change she will make will be as follows: She will put in 30 red chips and 10 white chips or vice versa—30 white chips and 10 red chips. Your assignment is to discover when she changes the population bag in either of these ways. The only method of investigation you are allowed is to pull out 10 chips on each trial. After you have pulled out the 10 chips, you must state whether or not the population bag is *different*; that is, whether or not, on this trial, the CPA has changed the number of each kind of chip.

Now, imagine what happens during one trial. The chips are in the bag; the bag is shaken up. You reach in, without looking, and pull out 10 chips. Your strategy will be, of course, to examine the 10 chips you pull out. If 6 are red and 4 are white, do you suspect the population bag has been changed? That result, 6-plus-4, could easily have occurred even if the population bag still had an equal number

of red and white chips in it, don't you agree? What if you pulled out 9 red chips and only 1 white (call this a 9-plus-1 result)? *Then* would you declare that you suspected a change in the population bag? You probably would *because such a result would be unlikely if there had been no change.* Notice that the 9-plus-1 result would only have been *unlikely,* not *impossible.* You *could* have pulled out 9 red and 1 white chip from the 20-20 mixture of red and white chips, but you wouldn't expect this to happen very often.

You can see that there are two kinds of mistakes you could make. One is declaring that you detect a change when there really has not been a change: this is a *Type I error.* Had you declared a change on the basis of your 6-plus-4 sample, you might have made a Type I error. The other mistake would be to declare *no* change when in fact there *had* been a change. Call this a Type II error. If you ignored the 9-plus-1 evidence of your sample and declared no change, you would run the risk of making a Type II error.

Now that you know how to play the game answer these questions: *What samples would make you declare that a change has taken place? What samples would make you declare no change?* Before you answer you will probably want to know the penalties for making a Type I or Type II error. Suppose the scoring rules are such that you must pay the CPA a sum of money each time you make a Type I error, but only half as much if you make a Type II error. Both errors are bad, but Type I is more costly. In this case, you would want to avoid declaring a change when there has not been a change. That is, because it carries a bigger penalty you will try to avoid Type I errors. Say you decide that you do not want to make this mistake more than 5 times in 100 trials. (Yes, 5 times out of 100 is the conventional .05 significance level mentioned in many statistical procedures.) Notice, however, that the more you try to avoid making Type I errors, the more likely you will be to make Type II errors. The more reluctant you are to declare a change, the more likely it is that you will fail to declare a change when there is one.

Now, what if the stakes were very high and you wanted to play the game as well as possible. Is there some way you could *prepare* for the game? One way would be to rehearse: Prepare for yourself a bag with the 40 chips in it, 20 red and 20 white, and pull out a whole series of samples of 10, recording the composition of each sample before returning it to the bag. You could graph this information, as in Figure 1, placing an x in the proper place each time you pulled out that kind of sample.

Of the 9 trials displayed by the graph, only one showed a result that looks unbalanced—the 3-plus-7. Suppose you ran

100 trials like this and graphed the distribution of results. And suppose you found that the 9-plus-1 or 1-plus-9 result showed up *only twice.* You would use this result to help you formulate your strategy. You would think to yourself:

```
When I'm playing the game, if I pull out
a 9-plus-1 sample, I'm going to declare
that I detect a change in the population
bag because on the basis of my 100
trials, I can see that 9-plus-1 is highly
unusual when the bag contains the 20-20
mixture. In my 100 trials, 9-plus-1 only
occurred twice, so it looks as if I only
have a 2 out of 100 or 2% chance of being
wrong. This is a Type I error--saying
there's been a change when there hasn't--
but the chance of that error is only 2%.
The 9-plus-1 result is very likely to be
due to a real change in the population bag.
```

Social scientists take advantage of a similar strategy when they use statistical tests. Remember what you have done: You *set up* for yourself the bag population that is most likely to occur and whose presence or absence you want to detect. Then you figured out the sample types you tend to draw when that population is the true one. Well, scientists imagine some particular state of the universe about which they want to experiment and construct a graph of the results that experiments with *samples* would produce if that state of things were indeed *true.* What they most often imagine for the purpose of doing statistics is that their experiment has had no effect, or that the correlation they are looking for is zero, just as you assumed *no change* in the population bag. For them, as for you, the no difference situation is the one against which to compare the results from particular samples.

For instance, when the t-test to detect the significance of the difference found between sample *means* is used, the experimentor starts with the assumption that there is no difference between the means of two populations of people. It has been shown that the *graph* of possible differences to be found among samples when *no* population difference exists—a graph similar to yours in Figure 1—matches a classic statistical distribution called t. This graph has been worked out by statisticians. The t distribution tells the scientist the probability of finding the difference produced by his samples in the event that no difference exists between the populations those samples represent.

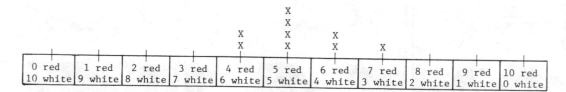

Figure 1. Occurrences of red and white chips during each of nine rehearsal trials when the population contains 20 red and 20 white chips

Now if *you* undertake a study for which the t-test is appropriate, you convert the score difference between the groups you have tested to a t-value, then look at the graph or table of t-values to find out the likelihood that your particular t would have occurred if there were no real difference between the populations your groups represent.

In summary, use of statistical tests follows this logic:

1. Let us start with the *tentative assumption* that the study we are doing—a correlation or experiment, or whatever—is looking for a result that, in truth, simply is not the case. No correlation or difference between groups exists.

2. Given this, let us decide what a graph of the results of many, many such studies would look like.

3. Then, let us do our study, and . . .

4. . . . Ask the question: *According to this graph, how likely is the result we have obtained?* If this graph says that it is *highly unlikely,* then we will chance the conclusion that there really *is* a correlation or difference between means, or whatever. We will say that we have found statistical significance.

What is meant by *highly unlikely* depends, as in your poker chips game, on the penalties encountered with a Type I error. If an announcement that the result found is statistically significant will be fraught with social, economic or professional reprisals, then stringent criteria for declaring statistical significance will be in order. If significance is proclaimed only when an obtained result could be expected 1% of the time or less, then strong protection against a Type I error has been provided. The person conducting the study has chosen the *.01 level.*[7]

You must be thinking that setting such a stringent criterion for producing significance will cause a lot of Type II errors, failing to detect a real change. That is correct. The more you avoid Type I errors, the more likely you will be to commit Type II errors. Suppose you decided that despite this drawback you want to keep to a probability of .05; that is, you cannot afford more than a 5% risk of a Type I error. Given that condition, *what could be done to give you a better chance of detecting a change if there were one?* How could the game be changed? This is a question about increasing the *power* of each trial.[8] In your game, the power of a trial is the chance you have on that trial of detecting a real change. Now, how could the game be changed to allow you increased power on each trial? There are two ways the power of a trial might be increased:

1. You could pull out a *larger sample*—maybe 20 instead of just 10 chips. At one extreme, you could examine all 40 chips. You would have 100% power, a 100% chance of finding a difference if there were one. At the other extreme, if you could only pull out 2 or 3 chips, you would find it almost impossible to make correct statements about whether or not the population bag had been changed.

2. The *actual* change in the population bag could be more drastic. Suppose your CPA promised that when she made a change, it would not just be from the even mix of 20-plus-20 to the slightly uneven 10-plus-30. Instead the change would be larger: say she decided to put in 5 red and 35 white or vice versa. You can see right away that such a large change would almost certainly show up even in your small sample of 10 chips. The larger the *actual* change in the population bag, the more apparent this will be in almost every sample.

It has been traditional in education and psychology to choose a Type I error rate of only 5%, that is, to set $\alpha = .05$. This means you will fail to detect some real changes. But you will fail to detect real changes *less often* if you use large samples, or if the population change, the effect you are looking for, is large when compared with the sampling variation in the data.

What to do with significant and nonsignificant results

The statistical worksheets contained in this book generally direct you to use a .05 or .10 probability level for Type I error. This means that you will declare an observed difference significant of its likelihood of occurrence would be fewer than 5 or 10 times in 100, were there no actual difference. The 5% and 10% *tables* are provided with the worksheets in this chapter to give you quick access to the levels most often used. Besides, the 5% level, as a general rule, is probably the best to use in most circumstances: it will keep you from overinterpreting small differences and encourage you to increase power by using adequate numbers. What is more important, if you have a result which makes a big difference—a large change or effect—then you will not need to worry about the statistical tests. They will back you up.

At this point you might ask: *What happens to the large number of results that do not meet the stringent .05 significance requirement?* In scientific reports, these are designated *not significant* and that is the end of it. But recent years have produced considerable debate about the appropriateness of a .05 cutoff line for deciding whether a result in non-research field studies should be considered important. What about observed differences that have, say, only a .15 probability of occurrence in the absence of a true difference? This is still a fairly rare result.

Besides, evaluation presents precisely the sort of situation where such results might be useful. This is because, in evaluation, results of statistical tests are seldom the sole determiners of a decision. Rather, they serve as one piece of evidence among a sometimes complex set of considerations. When put to such non-scientific uses, results from evaluation studies should probably not be required to meet strin-

---

7. Explanation of some vocabulary is in order here: the initial *tentative assumption* described here is called by statisticians the *null hypothesis,* the supposition of no change or difference. The size of the risk of Type I error chosen is called *Alpha* (α), and the decimal expressing this is referred to in statistical conversations as the study's *Alpha level.* The risk of a Type II error is referred to as *Beta* (β).

8. Something to think about to show whether you have absolutely mastered this information: *Power* = $1-\beta$. But β does not equal $1-\alpha$. Finding β depends on knowing the true difference . . . but these ideas are quite advanced, and not at all necessary for dealing with the statistics in this book.

gent significance criteria. It will suffice to accompany a report of any obtained difference with an estimate of its probability of occurrence if no true difference exists. The *users* of the information can then decide how seriously the result should be taken.

Suppose you find, for example, that a particular experimental mathematics program produces at the end of a school year a 10-point achievement advantage over a control program. A t-test for the difference between means may show that the 10-point difference would have occurred 20 times out of 100 if there were *no* actual difference between achievement effects of the two programs (p = .20). This means that were you to repeat this same study and if the experimental program were indeed ineffective, you'd get a difference of 10 points or more only 1 time in every 5. Reporting the .20 likelihood of the t-value computed by the test provides a more fair evaluation of the program than does a simple statement of nonsignificance. Nonsignificance makes the program sound conclusively ineffective, when actually the result was a fairly large difference in the predicted direction! Viewed in this way, and weighed among other considerations, the result might well affect the user's choice whether to continue, change, modify, or scrap the program.

You are advised, then, to *report* your nonsignificant results, accompanied by their greater-than-.05 probability of Type I error. You can find tables for estimating the actual probability of your results at the back of most statistics texts; and since using these tables could require interpolation, you might need a data analyst to help you.

The educational significance of statistically significant results

Just as you should not view *nonsignificant* results as conclusive evidence of program ineffectiveness, you should not be so awestruck by *significant* results that you fail to see them clearly within the context of the evaluation questions you are trying to answer. Even if you have found that the experimental group produced a significantly higher mean score than the control group, or if schools with a certain characteristic perform significantly better than schools with another, you will still need to decide about the *educational* significance of your findings. To put it bluntly: *So what?*

Statistical significance, after all, only tells you whether or not the results of your particular evaluation or experiment can be safely attributed to a *real* change in participating groups. Given the number of cases, and the variability you found in the scores, your result was of too great a magnitude to be due to chance.

However, statistical significance does not tell you anything about how *valuable* the difference was. For one thing, *statistical* significance is heavily dependent on the number of students or classes in your groups. If you have a large number of cases, even small correlations or minimal differences between means might show significance. A program which taught a large number of E-group students, say 300, to answer correctly two more items than the control group could answer might show a statistically significant superiority. But is learning two more facts in the course of a year

educationally significant? And if the program cost more, was it worth it?

As you can see, achievement of significant or nonsignificant results is only the beginning of data interpretation. How you report your findings will depend on requirements established by your audience's information needs, sophistication, and desire for fairness.

How To Find the Proper Procedure in This Chapter for Examining Differences Between Group Scores

Before proceeding, you will need to decide whether you need Section I or II of this chapter. If the groups you will be comparing have been *matched,* then use Section II; if they are *unmatched,* use Section I.

You have *matched* groups if each *case* for which you have a score in one group—usually a student since matching works best when assigning students to programs—can be matched with a case in the *other* group based on some characteristic which makes them likely to produce similar results on the outcome measure. Perhaps the matched students are alike because they had the same or nearly the same pretest scores; or perhaps they have the same IQ, or are from the same socio-economic background, or maybe they have a combination of these things in common. Evaluations or experiments using randomized groups consisting of members who were *matched before random assignment occurred* yield highly credible results. This is because matching allows you to build a strong argument that the groups were initially equivalent in most important characteristics. Any difference in outcomes, then, can be attributed easily to the program or experimental treatment.

You can use matched groups statistics in one of three situations:

1. At the time of assignment of students to programs, a matched pairs[9] method of randomizing was used.

2. You are testing for a statistically significant difference between posttest and pretest scores produced by the *same* group, answering the question: *Was the gain from pretest to posttest statistically significant?* In this case, each student's posttest score will be matched with *his own* pretest score.

3. You have decided to form *non-equivalent* control and experimental groups by matching students who cannot be assigned to programs randomly—because, for example, they must remain within a particular classroom or school. Selection of matched pairs proceeds in the same way as for the randomized procedure, except that group membership is otherwise determined. This procedure, called *post hoc matching,* can occur either before or after the program has taken place. Post hoc matching is frowned upon by some evaluation theorists because it is difficult to know whether significant effects have resulted from the program or from other systematic

9. These methods are described in most texts on experimental design and educational research. See, for instance: Fitz-Gibbon, C. T., & Morris, L. L. How to design a program evaluation. In L. L. Morris (Ed.), *Program evaluation kit.* Beverly Hills: Sage Publications, 1978.

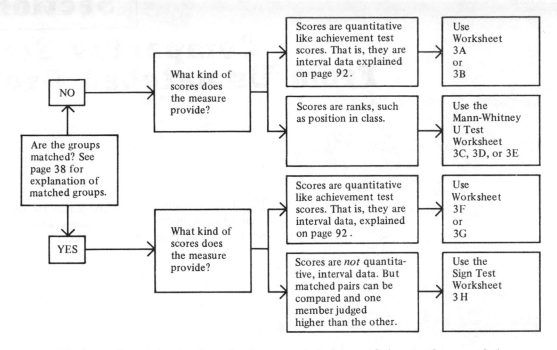

Figure 2. Decision tree for selecting a statistical test of the significance of the difference between outcomes from two groups

group differences. The procedure *does* give comparative information valuable for interpreting your results, however, and is justifiable when you can show that the groups you are comparing were so alike initially that they might as well have been randomly composed.

If you *cannot* pair the scores of one group with those of another, then use Section I which prescribes statistics for comparing results from *unmatched* groups.

Once you have decided whether the groups you are comparing are matched or unmatched, use Figure 2 to choose an appropriate worksheet. If the figure allows you a choice between performing a test of statistical significance and estimating confidence limits, and if you feel your

audience will understand them, choose confidence limits. The introduction to each worksheet will help you interpret and report the result it produces. Before you become involved with worksheets, pay attention to the next section.

Remember To Graph Results

Do not neglect the first critical step in data analysis: display the raw scores graphically. Whenever you intend to compare scores from two groups, plot the score distributions, by hand or typewriter, in a way that makes it easy to catch a profile of each group's performance. Below are two examples of how to display the distributions of posttest scores from an experimental group and a control group.

Example 1

Example 2

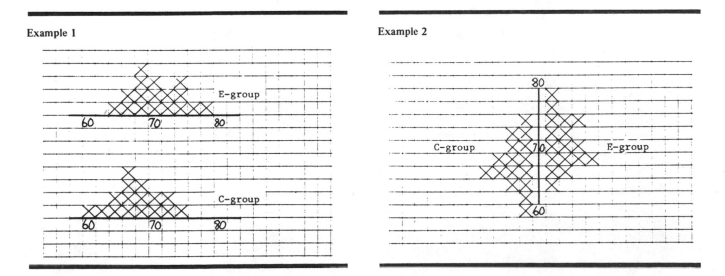

Section I

Comparing Scores
From Unmatched Groups

Use these worksheets when comparing the mean scores of unmatched groups. The groups being compared may or may not have the same number of members.

Testing the Statistical Significance of the Difference Between Two Means: The t-test for Unmatched Groups

The t-test is a test to see if there *is* a statistically significant difference between the mean scores of two groups—say, an experimental (E) group and a control (C) group. Demonstrating whether or not a difference is statistically significant is important: a statistical test tells you how frequently your result would be expected to occur simply by chance if indeed there were no real difference in E-group and C-group performance. A difference that a statistical test determines to be *not* significant must be considered too small and chancy to be taken seriously. Some of the logic underlying the *t-test* of significance is explained in the following paragraphs.

Suppose a group of students comprising a class have all been taught in the same way all year. You arrive in April and randomly divide the class into two subgroups, giving both the same test. You would not expect to find that the scores of the two random subgroups are very different. On the other hand, the mean scores of these subgroups are not likely to be *exactly* the same either. Because all scores are susceptible to errors and variability, any two sets of test scores—even from essentially the same group—will have slightly different means. Just *how* different the two means turn out to be will depend upon:

1. The sizes of the subgroups. The larger the number in each subgroup, the more you can expect the mean of each subgroup to be the same as the mean of the whole original group.
2. The variability of the scores. The wider the variation you find among the scores, the more likely it is that the means will be, by chance selection, quite a bit different.

The t-test is designed to help you take into account these two factors—group size and score variability—when interpreting the difference you have observed between groups. If a t-test were applied in the situation just described, you would expect it to show that, given the variability of scores in the two groups, the difference between means was *not* big enough to reach statistical significance. You would conclude that the two subgroups were not really different.

Now, suppose that a group of students has been divided randomly into two groups. One has been taught by what you have been told is a good method, and the other group has been taught by a method that you suspect to be much poorer. Again, you give a test, and find the means for the two groups. Sure enough, as expected, one group has a higher mean score than the other. But you have to consider the possibility that this difference was due to chance—that the two groups are in reality performing equivalently. Only by first ruling out this possibility will you be able to consider the difference in results worth mentioning.

One way to see if the difference is too large to be just a chance fluke would be to pool all the scores from both groups and keep selecting random subgroups and recording the difference between the means. If the differences between pairs of groups obtained in this way were smaller than the difference found when you divided the students according to how they were taught, then you would conclude that teaching method had really made a difference. This procedure would work well, but it would be very time-consuming.

The t-test is a quick way of accomplishing the same end by applying what amounts to the same procedure. It answers the question: Is the *obtained* difference between the means bigger than the differences you would expect to obtain if the two groups were actually equivalent? In other words, is the difference you obtained bigger than the differences which could be expected to occur by chance sampling variation?

To apply a t-test to the difference between means, you calculate an *obtained t-value* by inserting into a formula the obtained difference between means and its associated standard deviation, representing the variability of scores. You then check the obtained t-value against a *tabled t-value*. The tabled t-value is read from a table organized according to the number of cases in each group. If the obtained t-value is larger than the tabled t-value, this means the obtained difference between means is larger than would be expected if the groups were not really different.

When To Use the t-test

The t-test is most often used in conjunction with research and evaluation designs to scrutinize differences in scores—achievement, attitude or whatever—between experimental and control groups. You might want to use a t-test to check if *pretest* scores of two randomly composed groups are equivalent, that is, as an indicator of whether randomization has worked. The two groups can be considered equivalent if the obtained t-value is *less* than the tabled t-value. This indicates *absence* of a statistically significant difference on the measure used. A true, randomly selected, control group will almost always turn out to be equivalent to the randomly selected experimental group. In the case where you are using a *non-equivalent control group*—one *not* formed by random assignment—a test for significant pretest differences is essential. Conclusions about the final effects of a program will be strengthened if a t-test of the difference between E- and C-group *pretest means* shows *no* statistical significance. This indicates the E- and C-groups probably started out equivalent in achievement, attitudes, or whatever.

You should compute a t-test to check if the difference in *posttest* scores between two groups, usually an E- and a C-group, is statistically significant.

The t-test has non-design uses as well, all of them situations where you want to know if score differences between two groups on some measure are significant. You might want to test, for example, whether boys and girls are achieving equally well in a certain reading program. A t-test will tell if the boys' mean score is significantly different from the girls' mean score. You can use a t-test to examine the difference between *attitudes* of certain parent groups or between *program implementation* practices at different sites.

In general you can use a t-test to search out statistically significant differences between any two groups you can identify on any measure you can administer—though how you *interpret* the results will differ from one situation to another. There is one qualification to this sweeping statement, however: the t-test is most appropriate for determining the significance of the difference between means *when the number of participants in each of the two groups is about equal.* If the group sizes are quite *un*equal (say if one group is more than 20% larger than the other), then look at the standard deviation associated with each group's mean before using the t-test. If the standard deviations are similar, go ahead with the t-test. If they are quite different, you should probably use the Mann-Whitney U Test (Worksheets 3C, D, and E) instead of or in addition to the t-test. Alternatively, you could make the numbers per group equal by randomly removing scores from the larger group so that it equals the size of the smaller group, and then performing the t-test with only the data from these equalized groups.

Note, as well, that the t-test does not tell you whether or not a statistically significant difference is an *important* difference. You or your evaluation audience will have to judge this for yourselves by examining differences and asking if they are large enough to be considered important educationally.

Worksheet 3A

Testing the Statistical Significance of the Difference Between Two Means: The t·test for Unmatched Groups

Steps	Example

PREVIEW

Below is a formula for t. The following steps explain how to calculate t using this formula. When you have a value for t, called your _obtained_ _t-value_, you will compare it with a value in a table which is provided in the worksheet. If your obtained t is larger than the _tabled t_, then the difference between the means is statistically significant.

$$t = \frac{\overline{x}_E - \overline{x}_C}{s_d} \quad \text{where}$$

$\overline{x}_E$ = E-group mean

$\overline{x}_C$ = C-group mean

s_d = a standard deviation, read as "s sub d," the same s_d as calculated in Worksheet 3B

Background

The students in one classroom were randomly assigned to cover the semester's social studies by one of two methods: projects or regular classwork. Those working in the projects method were the E-group, and those doing regular class-work were called the C-group. At the end of the semester, they all took a 50-item test on the social studies curriculum.

Step 1. Prepare input data

For each group, compute the mean score, $\overline{x}$, and the standard deviation, s, and record these values in the Descriptive Statistics Table below along with the number, n, of scores of each group. As you work through the following pages, you will be able to refer back to this table if you forget what quantity a symbol stands for.

Descriptive Statistics Table

	Mean of scores	Standard deviation	Number of scores
E-group	$\overline{x}_E =$	$s_E =$	$n_E =$
C-group	$\overline{x}_C =$	$s_C =$	$n_C =$

Step 1. Prepare input data

The Descriptive Statistics Table shows that the 12 E-group students had a mean score of 30 on the posttest, and the 15 C-group students had a mean score of 36. Thus the C-group students had a higher mean score.

Descriptive Statistics Table

	Mean of scores	Standard deviation	Number of scores
E-group	$\overline{x}_E = 30$	$s_E = 6$	$n_E = 12$
C-group	$\overline{x}_C = 36$	$s_C = 4$	$n_C = 15$

Steps	Example

Step 2. Compute $\bar{x}_E - \bar{x}_C$, the difference between group means

Subtract the mean of the C-group from the mean of the E-group and record the result here:

☐ $= \bar{x}_E - \bar{x}_C$

Step 3. Compute s_d

$$s_d = \sqrt{\left[\frac{s_E^2(n_E-1) + s_C^2(n_C-1)}{n_E + n_C - 2}\right]\left[\frac{1}{n_E} + \frac{1}{n_C}\right]}$$

Here are ten substeps for computing s_d using an electronic calculator. The procedure first produces the values that belong inside each square bracket; then it multiplies these quantities and takes the square root.

a. Multiply s_E by itself. Then multiply the result by (n_E-1)--the number that is <u>one less</u> than the number of scores in the E-group. Put the result here:

☐ $= s_E^2(n_E-1)$

b. Multiply s_C by itself, and then multiply this result by (n_C-1). Put the result here:

☐ $= s_C^2(n_C-1)$

c. Add the results of Substep a and Substep b and put the sum here:

☐

d. Add n_E and n_C and subtract 2 from the sum. Put the result here:

☐ $= n_E + n_C - 2$

e. To produce the quantity inside the first square bracket in the equation, divide the result of Substep c by the result of Substep d. Put the result here:

☐

Step 2. Compute $\bar{x}_E - \bar{x}_C$, the difference between group means

30 − 36 =   -6

Step 3. Compute s_d

a.

6 X 6 X 11 =   396

b.

4 X 4 X 14 =   224

c.

396 + 224 =   620

d.

12 + 15 − 2 =   25

e.

$\frac{620}{25}$ =   24.6

Steps	Example

f. Now, enter 1 on the calculator. Divide it by n_E and put the result here:

$$\boxed{} = \frac{1}{n_E}$$

g. Enter 1 on the calculator. Divide it by n_C and put the result here:

$$\boxed{} = \frac{1}{n_C}$$

h. To produce the quantity inside the second square bracket in the equation, add the results of Substeps f and g and put the sum here:

$$\boxed{} = \frac{1}{n_E} + \frac{1}{n_C}$$

i. Now multiply the result of Substep e by the result of Substep h. Enter the result here:

$$\boxed{}$$

j. Find the square root of Substep i. This is s_d. Enter it here:

$$\boxed{} = s_d$$

Step 4. Compute t

Divide the result of Step 2 by the result of Step 3, Substep j. This value is your obtained t-value. Enter it here:

$$\boxed{} = \text{obtained t-value}$$

Notice that if $\bar{x}_E - \bar{x}_C$ was negative, your obtained t-value will be negative.

Example

f.

$$\frac{1}{12} = \boxed{0.08}$$

g.

$$\frac{1}{15} = \boxed{0.07}$$

h.

$$0.08 + 0.07 = \boxed{0.15}$$

i.

$$(24.6)\,(0.15) = \boxed{3.72}$$

j.

$$\sqrt{3.72} = 1.93$$

$$s_d = \boxed{1.93}$$

Step 4. Compute t

Obtained t-value =

$$\frac{-6}{1.93} = \boxed{-3.11}$$

Steps	Example

Step 5. Find the tabled t-value

Tabled t-values

Column 1 n_1+n_2-2	Column 2 If you predicted which group would do better	Column 3 If you didn't pre-dict which group would do better (or were wrong)
6	1.94	2.45
7	1.89	2.36
8	1.86	2.31
9	1.83	2.26
10	1.81	2.23
11	1.80	2.20
12	1.78	2.18
13	1.77	2.16
14	1.76	2.14
15	1.75	2.13
16	1.75	2.12
17	1.74	2.11
18	1.73	2.10
19	1.73	2.09
20	1.72	2.09
21	1.72	2.08
22	1.72	2.07
23	1.71	2.07
24	1.71	2.06
25	1.71	2.06
26	1.71	2.06
27	1.70	2.05
28	1.70	2.05
29	1.70	2.04
30	1.70	2.04
40	1.68	2.02
60	1.67	2.00
120	1.66	1.98
∞*	1.64	1.96

*The infinity sign, ∞, denotes in this case any number greater than 120.

This table is taken from Table III of Fisher and Yates: <u>Statistical Tables for Biological, Agri-cultural and Medical Research</u>, published by Longman Group Ltd., London (previously published by Oliver and Boyd, Edinburgh), and by permission of the authors and publishers.

To find your tabled t-value from the table above:

a. Choose between Column 2 and Column 3. If you believed that one group would score higher than the other (e.g., that the E-group would outperform the C-group) and it did, then use Column 2. If you predicted that one group would do better but it did not, then use Column 3 to see if this unexpected result was perhaps mere chance. If you made no predic-tion either way, use Column 3.

Step 5. Find the tabled t-value

Tabled t-values

Column 1 n_1+n_2-2	Column 2 If you predicted which group would do better	Column 3 If you didn't pre-dict which group would do better (or were wrong)
6	1.94	2.45
7	1.89	2.36
8	1.86	2.31
9	1.83	2.26
10	1.81	2.23
11	1.80	2.20
12	1.78	2.18
13	1.77	2.16
14	1.76	2.14
15	1.75	2.13
16	1.75	2.12
17	1.74	2.11
18	1.73	2.10
19	1.73	2.09
20	1.72	2.09
21	1.72	2.08
22	1.72	2.07
23	1.71	2.07
24	1.71	2.06
25	1.71	(2.06)
26	1.71	2.06
27	1.70	2.05
28	1.70	2.05
29	1.70	2.04
30	1.70	2.04
40	1.68	2.02
60	1.67	2.00
120	1.66	1.98
∞	1.64	1.96

a. The teacher conducted this experimental com-parison of projects with regular classwork in order to see which worked better. He had <u>not</u> made a prediction as to which method would work best, so he used Column 3.

Steps	Example

b. Find in the first column the value that you calculated for $n_E + n_C - 2$ in Step 3, Substep d, or the nearest number to that value.

b. $n_E + n_C - 2 = 25$

Therefore, the row beginning 25 was underlined.

c. Find the number which is on the row you just selected and in the column you just chose in Substep a above. This is your tabled t-value. Enter it here:

```
┌──────────┐
│          │  = tabled t-value
└──────────┘
```

c. The Column 3 number on the row underlined is 2.06.

tabled t-value = ⟦ 2.06 ⟧

Step 6. Interpret the statistic

The obtained t-value may have been negative. Ignore the negative sign if there is one, and compare the absolute size of the obtained t-value with the tabled t-value. If the obtained value is larger than the tabled value, then the difference between the two groups was statistically significant in the conventional sense. If you used Column 2, you can say that the difference was significant on a "5% one-tailed test"; if you used Column 3, the difference was significant on a "5% two-tailed test."

If the obtained t-value was <u>not</u> larger than the tabled t-value, this indicates that the difference <u>could</u> have been the result of chance. You cannot regard the result as showing that either group did better than the other. You must conclude that "the difference between group means was not statistically significant."

Examine the educational significance of the result. If the E-group did better than the C-group, <u>how much</u> better? Did the average gain represent valuable extra learning or just a gain of a few items? Making such a judgment is often difficult. Meet with administrators, staff, and possibly community members before you report your results to find out what magnitude of gain they would consider exciting.

Step 6. Interpret the statistic

Since 3.11 is larger than 2.06, the result was statistically significant. The C-group, doing regular classwork, had done significantly better than the E-group.

The teacher tentatively concluded that an advantage of 6 points in favor of the regular-classwork group, on a test of only 50 items, was indeed educationally significant. He thought, however, that the test, based on general concepts, might have given undue weight to aspects of the curriculum stressed most heavily by the regular program. Perhaps it neglected important learnings produced by working on projects.

Introduction to Worksheet 3B

Calculating the Confidence Limits for the Difference Between Two Means From Unmatched Groups

Suppose that you have in hand the results of an achievement test administered to two groups—a group (the E-group) which received a new experimental program and a control group (the C-group) which received the usual program. You have calculated the means for each group and found the difference between the two means:

E-group mean = 80

C-group mean = 70

difference between means = 10

The E-group did 10 points better than the C-group. Now you will want to know how much confidence you can place in a difference of 10 points: *If you repeated the program next year with similar conditions and similar students, would you be likely to get the same difference between the means?* How sure can you be, in other words, that this result is showing you a real difference caused by something in the programs, and not a mere unrepeatable happenstance?

The procedure described by Worksheet 3A will enable you to say something like this:

```
The difference we could expect if we
repeated the evaluation study might be as
small as 3 points or it could be as large
as 17 points; it will almost certainly be
somewhere within the range:  10 ± 7. [10]
```

Confidence limits not only give you a good idea of the range of likely outcomes, they also provide a test of the statistical significance of the obtained difference between two groups. To see why this is so, consider the situation in which the lower confidence limit is negative. Suppose, for example, that instead of 10 ± 7, the confidence limits you obtained had been 10 ± 12. The *upper* confidence limit would be an outcome in which the E-group scored better than the C-group by 22 points; but the *lower* confidence limit would be -2, a potential difference between group means in which the C-group actually does better than the E-group by 2 points! The important thing to notice in this case is that *the confidence limits span zero*. This means that

the difference between the means might, with a certain selected probability, have turned out to be zero. Whenever the confidence limits include zero within their range, there is *no* statistically significant difference between the means. In these cases, *chance* may be responsible for the particular difference between the groups obtained on this one test administration. Next time the *C-group* might score higher.

When To Use Confidence Limits

When reporting the difference between means, use either a t-test such as the one described by Worksheet 3A to determine statistical significance, *or* use confidence limits. Confidence limits are preferable in most cases, particularly if you plan to discuss the *size* of the difference between the means—nearly always of interest in program evaluation where your concern will be not only *whether* but *how much* difference a program or treatment has made. Besides, confidence limits usually are easier to explain to lay audiences than are statistics that involve calculating a number foreign to the data at hand, such as a t-value or a Mann-Whitney U.

If the E-group did better than the C-group, you should calculate confidence limits to see whether you could expect similar results in the future. If at first glance the C-group seems to have done better than the E-group, then it could be that the experimental program not only failed to improve things, but might have even caused harm. Before making this conclusion, calculate the confidence limits. Perhaps the confidence limits will include zero, indicating that zero, or *no difference,* was equally as likely as the result you got. In this case, the calculation of confidence limits shows that the lower E-group score was probably just due to chance, not a significant one.

Note that although the terms E-group and C-group are used in this discussion and in the worksheet, you might be comparing two experimental programs or two groups defined by something other than the program they have received, for instance, sex, age, or having had some experience. Remember, as well, that significance as judged by calculating confidence limits does not tell you whether or not an observed difference is *important.* You or your evaluation audience will have to judge this for yourselves by asking if it is large enough to be considered important educationally.

---

10. Read 10 ± 7 as *10 plus or minus 7.* Ten plus seven gives 17, the *upper confidence limit.* Ten minus seven gives 3, the *lower confidence limit* for this difference between the means.

Calculating the Confidence Limits for the Difference Between Two Means From Unmatched Groups

Steps	Example

Steps

PREVIEW

The confidence limits for d, the difference between the means, are

$d + (t)(s_d)$ and $d - (t)(s_d)$ where

d = the difference between means you have obtained

s_d = the standard deviation, read as "s sub d," of the distribution of all d's that could have occurred by chance

t = a number chosen from a table--t takes into account how confident you want to be and how many scores you are working with

It is not necessary for you to understand s_d and t. It is merely necessary that you calculate them for use with the statistical test.

Step 1. Start with a table like the one below, filling in for each group these values: mean, standard deviation, and number of scores

	Mean of scores	Standard deviation	Number of scores
E-group	$\overline{x}_E$ =	s_E =	n_E =
C-group	$\overline{x}_C$ =	s_C =	n_C =

The subscripts E and C are used so that you can keep track of which mean, standard deviation, and number of scores belong to the Experimental group, and which belong to the Control.

Step 2. Calculate d, the difference between means

Subtract the C-group mean from the E-group mean. The result is the difference between means, d.

$d = \begin{bmatrix} \text{E-group} \\ \text{mean} \end{bmatrix} - \begin{bmatrix} \text{C-group} \\ \text{mean} \end{bmatrix}$

Example

Background

Forty-five mathematics classes had been randomly assigned to an experimental program which used new procedures and materials and to a control program based on a slight update of a district's former methods. At the end of one semester, a district-developed test was administered to all students. The average score for each mathematics class was calculated. Then these class scores were averaged. The experimental classes had a mean classroom score of 80 compared with a mean classroom score of 70 for C-group classes.

Step 1. Table of input data

	Mean of scores	Standard deviation	Number of scores
E-group	$\overline{x}_E$ = 80	s_E = 8	n_E = 20
C-group	$\overline{x}_C$ = 70	s_C = 6	n_C = 25

Step 2. Calculate d, the difference between means

d = 80 - 70

  = 10

Steps	Example

Step 3. Calculate s_d

The standard deviation of the distribution of d's, s_d, is computed by the following formula.

$$s_d = \sqrt{\left[\frac{s_E^2(n_E-1) + s_C^2(n_C-1)}{n_E + n_C - 2}\right]\left[\frac{1}{n_E} + \frac{1}{n_C}\right]}$$

Here are ten substeps for computing s_d using an electronic calculator. The procedure first produces the values that belong inside each square bracket; then it multiplies these quantities and takes the square root.

a. Multiply s_E by itself to obtain s_E^2. Then multiply this by (n_E-1), that is, by one less than the number of scores in the E-group. Put the result here:

   $= s_E^2(n_E-1)$

b. Multiply s_C by itself, and then multiply this result by (n_C-1). Put the result here:

[ ] $= s_C^2(n_C-1)$

c. Add the results of Substep a and Substep b and put the sum here:

[ ]

d. Add n_E and n_C and subtract 2 from the sum. Put the result here:

[ ] $= n_E + n_C - 2$

e. To produce the quantity inside the first bracket in the equation, divide the result of Substep c by the result of Substep d. Put the result here:

[ ]

f. Now, enter 1 on the calculator. Divide it by n_E and put the result here:

   $= \frac{1}{n_E}$

Step 3. Calculate s_d

a.

8 x 8 x (20-1) =   [1216]

b.

6 x 6 x (25-1) =   [864]

c.

1216 + 864 =   [2080]

d.

20 + 25 - 2 =   [43]

e.

$\frac{2080}{43} =$ [48.37]

f.

$\frac{1}{20} =$ [0.05]

Steps	Example

g. Enter 1 on the calculator. Divide it by n_C and put the result here:

$$\boxed{} = \frac{1}{n_C}$$

h. To produce the quantity inside the second square bracket in the equation, add the results of Substeps f and g and put the sum here:

$$\boxed{} = \frac{1}{n_E} + \frac{1}{n_C}$$

i. Now multiply the result of Substep e by the result of Substep h. Enter the result here:

$$\boxed{}$$

j. Find the square root of Substep i. This is s_d. Enter it here:

$$\boxed{} = s_d$$

---

g.

$$\frac{1}{25} = \boxed{0.04}$$

h.

$$0.05 + 0.04 = \boxed{0.09}$$

i.

$$(48.37)\ (0.09) = \boxed{4.35}$$

j.

$$\sqrt{4.35} = 2.09$$

$$s_d = \boxed{2.09}$$

Step 4. Choose a t-value

Now you need a number called t. This value depends upon how many __cases__ there are in each group and on __how sure you want to be__ that the confidence limits you calculate include possible differences to be found between the groups if the study were repeated. To some extent, then, you have a choice among sizes of confidence limits to report. If you are not afraid of being wrong, for instance, you can calculate a narrow band of confidence limits. As the confidence limits you choose to report grow wider, however, you can be more certain that the true size of the difference between the groups lies within those limits-- but you also take a greater chance of including zero. Luckily, if your data are based on the scores of quite a few cases, you can have the best of both situations--you can produce a narrow range of confidence limits as well as high certainty of actually "capturing" the true difference.

Choose your value of t from the table on the following page. First go down the first column to the row which starts with the number that equals $n_E + n_C - 2$, the same number you calculated in Step 3d above. Then choose a t-value from that row, according to how sure you want to be about the boundaries. If you choose the 80% column, you will be able to say, "The difference between the means will lie within these boundaries," and expect to be correct four out of five times, or 80% of the time. In order for you to

---

Step 4. Choose a t-value

$$n_E + n_C - 2 = 43$$

The evaluator decided to use the conventional .05 level so he could report confidence limits with the statement that he was 95% sure that the difference would lie within the boundaries. The t-value he found from the table, therefore, was 2.02.

Steps	Example

be correct more times, like 95 times out of 100, the confidence limits would have to be further apart. Your choice of the 95% column would therefore lead to lower and upper confidence limits which are further away from each other.

n_1+n_2-2	4 out of 5 odds (80% confidence)	95 out of 100 odds (95% confidence)
6	1.44	2.45
7	1.41	2.36
8	1.40	2.31
9	1.38	2.26
10	1.37	2.23
11	1.36	2.20
12	1.36	2.18
13	1.35	2.16
14	1.35	2.14
15	1.34	2.13
16	1.34	2.12
17	1.33	2.11
18	1.33	2.10
19	1.33	2.09
20	1.32	2.09
21	1.32	2.08
22	1.32	2.07
23	1.32	2.07
24	1.32	2.06
25	1.32	2.06
30	1.31	2.04
40	1.30	2.02
60	1.30	2.00
120	1.29	1.98
∞*	1.28	1.96

*The infinity sign, ∞, denotes in this case any number greater than 120.

The third column, the .05 level, represents the conventional minimal level of certainty demanded by the social sciences. Some evaluation theorists have argued that it is too demanding for the large scale studies conducted by evaluators. In your situation, therefore, if a chance of being right four out of five times is good enough, then choose the 80% level. If your data, however, stand up under the 95% test, then by all means use it.

Step 5. Calculate confidence limits

a. Multiply the t-value selected in Step 4 by s_d which was calculated in Step 3. Enter the result here:

□ = (t)(s_d)

Example column:

n_1+n_2-2	4 out of 5 odds (80% confidence)	95 out of 100 odds (95% confidence)
6	1.44	2.45
7	1.41	2.36
8	1.40	2.31
9	1.38	2.26
10	1.37	2.23
11	1.36	2.20
12	1.36	2.18
13	1.35	2.16
14	1.35	2.14
15	1.34	2.13
16	1.34	2.12
17	1.33	2.11
18	1.33	2.10
19	1.33	2.09
20	1.32	2.09
21	1.32	2.08
22	1.32	2.07
23	1.32	2.07
24	1.32	2.06
25	1.32	2.06
30	1.31	2.04
40	1.30	2.02
60	1.30	2.00
120	1.29	1.98
∞	1.28	1.96

Step 5. Calculate confidence limits

a.

(2.02) (2.09) = 4.22

Steps	Example

b. To calculate the <u>upper</u> confidence limit, <u>add</u> the quantity just calculated in Substep a above to d, the difference between means. Enger the result here:

Upper confidence limit =

$$\boxed{} \quad = \quad d + (t)(s_d)$$

c. To calculate the <u>lower</u> confidence limit, <u>subtract</u> the quantity calculated in Substep a above from d, the difference between means.

Lower confidence limit =

$$\boxed{} \quad = \quad d - (t)(s_d)$$

Step 6. Interpret the statistic

<u>Does the confidence interval—that is, the range of values from the lower limit to the upper limit —include zero?</u> IF YES, the obtained difference between means could have been due to chance. The difference between the groups is not statistically significant.

IF NO, if both limits are positive or both are negative, then you can state with a certain amount of confidence—the odds you chose in selecting a t-value—that the difference between means could be expected to occur again in favor of the same group if the program were repeated. The obtained difference is statistically significant, not just due to chance. What this means is that there is a high probability that the same group would come out ahead if the same kind of study were performed again. You may want to say that a chance difference as large as the obtained d would be likely, having a probability of less than 20% if you chose the 80% column, or a probability of less than 5% if you chose the 95% column.

<u>Examine the educational significance of the results.</u> This involves interpreting the scale on which the results were based. If the E-group did better than the C-group, <u>how much</u> better? Did the average gain represent valuable extra learning or just a gain of a few items?

Confidence limits help you in these deliberations by revealing how great a difference you could expect from repeated studies of the same kind. Consider the lower confidence limit. Suppose it represents the true extent of the difference between the groups. Would you then conclude that one of the groups had a substantial educational advantage over the other? Now consider the upper confidence limit. Would you draw the same conclusion with respect to educational advantage?

---

b.

Upper confidence limit =

$10 + 4.22 = \boxed{14.22}$

c.

Lower confidence limit =

$10 - 4.22 = \boxed{5.78}$

Step 6. Interpret the statistic

The evaluator reported:

"The experimental classes generally achieved higher scores than the control group classes. The 20 E-group classes had an average score of 80 as compared with 70 for the C-group. This was a difference of 10 points in favor of the experimental group.

"The obtained difference was statistically significant (since both confidence limits were positive); that is, there is very little likelihood— less than 5% probability—that a difference as large as the obtained 10-point advantage for the E-group could have resulted from chance variation between the groups. It should be noted that the original decisions about which classes would form the E-group and which the C-group had been based on random assignment, and were therefore unbiased.

"The educational significance of the 10-point advantage of the E-group classes has been discussed by teachers involved in the program and district personnel who prepared the test. In terms of the confidence limits, the results point to an E-group advantage of between 6 and 14 points, approximately. Both the upper and lower limits were seen as a solid, promising start that justifies the expenditure of funds and effort that have gone into the new program, and merits its continuation."

Steps	Example
If you reach the same conclusion whether the upper or lower confidence limit is taken as the true difference between the groups, then the results of your study have provided you with a clear message. That message may point to one program's superiority or to a "tie score." On the other hand, if the upper confidence limit leads to one conclusion, and the lower confidence limit leads to the opposite conclusion, then you have no firm basis for decision-making.	

Introduction to Worksheets 3C, 3D, and 3E
Comparing Two Groups if the Outcome Measures are Ranks Rather Than Scores: The Mann-Whitney U Test

Like the t-test, the Mann-Whitney U Test helps you to determine whether your program or treatment has produced a significant difference between the performances of two groups on some measure. Unlike the t-test, the Mann-Whitney U statistic focuses on the *rank-ordering of cases,* rather than on means. It checks to see if there is a statistically significant difference between the rankings of one group's members as compared to those of the other group on the same measure. More precisely, it answers the question: *Is there a statistically significant difference between the two groups as displayed by the average ranks of their members?* The Mann-Whitney U Test compares the performance of two independent, *non-matched* groups whose members have been rank-ordered on the performance measure.

When To Use the Mann-Whitney U Test

Use the Mann-Whitney U Test rather than a t-test when your situation matches one of the following:

1. Your outcome measure does *not* yield quantitative scores—such as number correct, or rated strength of an expressed attitude—for which a mean can be computed. This is often the case when the measure involves a *qualitative* judgment, such as observers' opinions of the accuracy of implementation of a program, or teachers' ratings of the persuasiveness of student essays. Though it might be difficult to assign a *score* to such performances, observers, raters and readers can often place them into *ranked order* according to judged·quality.

2. Your outcome measure *can* be represented by a mean, but one group's size and the standard deviation of its scores are quite different from those of the other. These two conditions make the t-test inapplicable as was explained in the Introduction to Worksheet 3A.

This section contains three worksheets for the Mann-Whitney U Test. The first two are for situations in which the larger of the two groups contains at least 9 cases (students, perhaps, or classrooms) but fewer than 20. Worksheet 3C directs you in performing the U Test directly from ranked scores. Worksheet 3D accomplishes the same test, but shows you how to first convert quantitative scores to *ranks* in order to calculate U. Worksheet 3E is for situations where the larger group has more than 20 cases.[11]

Please remember that demonstration of statistical significance does not tell you whether or not the difference you have observed between groups is *important*. You or your evaluation audience will have to judge this for yourselves by asking whether it is large enough to be considered important educationally.

---

11. Should you have fewer than 9 cases in your larger group, consult: Popham, W. J. *Educational statistics: Use and interpretation.* New York: Harper and Row, 1967 (p. 305); or Siegel, S. *Non-parametric statistics for the behavioral sciences.* New York: McGraw Hill Book Co., 1956.

Worksheet 3C

The Mann-Whitney U Test:
For Use When There Are At Least 9 and
Not More Than 20 Cases in the Larger Group

Steps	Example

PREVIEW

A statistic to be calculated, called U, indicates how many times members of one group were outranked by members of the other group. The obtained U-value is compared with a value in a table to see if it is smaller than the tabled U-value. If it is smaller, then one group has ranked significantly higher than the other group.

Step 1. Start with a rank-group list

List ranks (1, 2, 3, etc.) in the left-hand column. In the right column, write the name of the group represented by the group member obtaining each rank.

Rank	Group membership
1	
2	
3	
4	
5	
.	
.	
.	
.	
n	

Background

The evaluator of a junior high science program was told that students had produced excellent projects in the new program, Program E. To check on this, the evaluator asked an independent judge to rank order the projects submitted to the annual Science Fair. The judge did not know which projects came from students in the new program or which came from the old program, Program C. From the judge's rank ordering, the evaluator was able to draw up a rank-group membership list.

Step 1. Start with a rank group list

Rank assigned to project	Science program of student who produced project E = new program C = old program
1	E
2	C
3	C
4	E
5	E
6	E
7	C
8	E
9	E
10	C
11	E
12	E
13	C
14	C
15	E

Steps	Example

Step 2. Record the numbers in the two groups, and add a third column to the rank-group list

a. Record the numbers in each group by counting from the second column of the rank-group membership list.

[   ] = Number of members in one group

[   ] = Number in the other group

b. Label the larger number n_L and call the group with the larger number of cases Group L.

[   ] = n_L (number in Group L)

c. Label the smaller number n_S and call the group with the smaller number of cases Group S.

[   ] = n_S (number in Group S)

d. Add a third column which indicates whether each case belonged to Group L or Group S. This simply means replacing the labels in the second column with L or S as appropriate.

Step 2. Record the numbers in the two groups, and add a third column to the rank-group list

a.

Number in Program E = 9

Number in Program C = 6

b.

$n_L = 9$

c.

$n_S = 6$

d.

Rank	Science program	Group
1	E	L
2	C	S
3	C	S
4	E	L
5	E	L
6	E	L
7	C	S
8	E	L
9	E	L
10	C	S
11	E	L
12	E	L
13	C	S
14	C	S
15	E	L

Steps	Example

Step 3. Going down the rank-group list, record the number of L's which precede each S score

Focus on the smaller group, Group S. Start at the top of the rank list, with the case representing the highest or best rank. Go down to the first time an S appears on the list. Next to the S, write how many L's have preceded it. Go on to the next S and repeat the process, counting all the L's preceding it, including those that were counted previously.

Step 3. Going down the rank-group list, record the number of L's which precede each S score

Rank	Science program	Group	Number of higher L's
1	E	L	
2	C	S	1
3	C	S	1
4	E	L	
5	E	L	
6	E	L	
7	C	S	4
8	E	L	
9	E	L	
10	C	S	6
11	E	L	
12	E	L	
13	C	S	8
14	C	S	8
15	E	L	

Step 4. Add up the numbers from Step 3 to find U

Add up the numbers you wrote next to the S's. Their total is U, the number of times the Group L students were ranked higher than the Group S students. Write it here:

$$\boxed{} = U$$

Step 4. Add up the numbers from Step 3 to find U

The total of the numbers in the fourth column of the table in Step 3 is 28.

$$U = \boxed{28}$$

Step 5. Calculate U'

Read U' as U prime.

$$U' = n_L \, n_S - U$$

To compute this, multiply n_S by n_L and subtract U from the answer.

$$\boxed{} = U'$$

Step 5. Calculate U'

$$U' = 9 \times 6 - 28$$
$$U' = 54 - 28$$
$$ = 26$$

$$U' = \boxed{26}$$

Step 6. Record U*

U* (read U star) is whichever value, U or U', is the **smaller**. Record not only the smaller value but also whether it was U or U'.

$$\boxed{} = U* = \boxed{}$$

value   U or U'

Step 6. Record U*

$$U* = \boxed{26} = U'$$

Steps	Example

Step 7. Find the tabled U* value

In the table below, find the column headed by the number in your larger group (n_L). Go down this column until you come to the row for the number in your smaller group (n_S).

Critical Values of U*
For a Two-Tailed Test at a = .10

n_S\n_L	9	10	11	12	13	14	15	16	17	18	19	20
1											0	0
2	1	1	1	2	2	2	3	3	3	4	4	4
3	3	4	5	5	6	7	7	8	9	9	10	11
4	6	7	8	9	10	11	12	14	15	16	17	18
5	9	11	12	13	15	16	18	19	20	22	23	25
6	12	14	16	17	19	21	23	25	26	28	30	32
7	15	17	19	21	24	26	28	30	33	35	37	39
8	18	20	23	26	28	31	33	36	39	41	44	47
9	21	24	27	30	33	36	39	42	45	48	51	54
10	24	27	31	34	37	41	44	48	51	55	58	62
11	27	31	34	38	42	46	50	54	57	61	65	69
12	30	34	38	42	47	51	55	60	64	68	72	77
13	33	37	42	47	51	56	61	65	70	75	80	84
14	36	41	46	51	56	61	66	71	77	82	87	92
15	39	44	50	55	61	66	72	77	83	88	94	100
16	42	48	54	60	65	71	77	83	89	95	101	107
17	45	51	57	64	70	77	83	89	96	102	109	115
18	48	55	61	68	75	82	88	95	102	109	116	123
19	51	58	65	72	80	87	94	101	109	116	123	130
20	54	62	69	77	84	92	100	107	115	123	130	138

Source: Table 7 from Auble, D., Extended tables for the Mann-Whitney statistic. *Bulletin of the Institute for Educational Research of Indiana University*, 1(2), 1953, with kind permission of the author.

Write this number here:

[ ] = Critical value of U*

Step 8. Compare the obtained U* value with the tabled U* value

Is the value of U* which you obtained in Step 6 smderer than the tabled U* value from Step 7?

- If yes, then you can state that one group is significantly higher than the other on the measure which ranked them.
- If no, then there is no statistically significant difference in the rankings of the two groups.

Step 7. Find the tabled U* value

n_S\n_L	⑨	10	11	12	13	14	15	16	17	18	19	20
1											0	0
2	1	1	1	2	2	2	3	3	3	4	4	4
3	3	4	5	5	6	7	7	8	9	9	10	11
4	6	7	8	9	10	11	12	14	15	16	17	18
5	9	11	12	13	15	16	18	19	20	22	23	25
⑥	→12←	14	16	17	19	21	23	25	26	28	30	32
7	15	17	19	21	24	26	28	30	33	35	37	39
8	18	20	23	26	28	31	33	36	39	41	44	47
9	21	24	27	30	33	36	39	42	45	48	51	54
10	24	27	31	34	37	41	44	48	51	55	58	62
11	27	31	34	38	42	46	50	54	57	61	65	69
12	30	34	38	42	47	51	55	60	64	68	72	77
13	33	37	42	47	51	56	61	65	70	75	80	84
14	36	41	46	51	56	61	66	71	77	82	87	92
15	39	44	50	55	61	66	72	77	83	88	94	100
16	42	48	54	60	65	71	77	83	89	95	101	107
17	45	51	57	64	70	77	83	89	96	102	109	115
18	48	55	61	68	75	82	88	95	102	109	116	123
19	51	58	65	72	80	87	94	101	109	116	123	130
20	54	62	69	77	84	92	100	107	115	123	130	138

Critical value of U* = [12]

Step 8. Compare the obtained U* value with the tabled U* value

U* is not smaller than the critical value. The difference between ranks received by Program E and Program C students was not statistically significant.

The evaluator reported the number of science projects submitted and indicated that students in both programs appeared to be producing projects of similar quality. He reported:

Steps	Example
For both statements, the test has left only a 10% chance of your statement being in error.	"Application of the Mann-Whitney U Test indicated no statistically significant difference between the average ranks of the two groups. Students from one group were not ranking higher than students from the other group to an extent which could be considered unlikely to occur by chance."

Steps:

For both statements, the test has left only a 10% chance of your statement being in error.

To summarize:

· If the obtained U* was greater than the tabled U*, neither group was significantly higher.

· If the obtained U* was smaller than the tabled U*, then, to decide which was the higher-ranked group, check back to Step 6:

If U* = U,   then the <u>smaller</u> group outranked the larger group

If U* = U', then the <u>larger</u> group outranked the smaller group

Example:

"Application of the Mann-Whitney U Test indicated no statistically significant difference between the average ranks of the two groups. Students from one group were not ranking higher than students from the other group to an extent which could be considered unlikely to occur by chance."

Had the obtained U value been smaller than the tabled U value, this would have implied, in this example, that Group E was ranking higher than Group C.

Worksheet 3D

The Mann-Whitney U Test: An Additional Example

Steps	Example

PREVIEW

This additional example has been included to show how scores can be changed to ranks and how tied ranks can be dealt with--before you calculate U.

Background

Students from two different reading programs entered a spelling competition. Their scores were:

Reading Program XX		Reading Program YY	
Peter	16	John	20
Janie	24	Susie	14
Tom	18	David	18
etc.	23	etc.	12
.	17	.	10
.	17	.	9
.	14	.	22
.	20	.	10
.	19	.	6
.	21		
.	15		

Step 1. Start with a rank-group list

To produce a rank-group list from scores, locate the top score and write 1 next to it, indicating first rank. Write 2 next to the second highest score, and continue down the list.

If scores are tied, assign the average rank. This can be quickly calculated. Suppose you come to one score with a rank of 7 and find 4 other scores which are the same, making a total of 5 tied scores. Then each of these scores must be assigned a rank of 9. That is,

$$7 + \frac{4}{2} = 7 + 2 = 9$$

To summarize this procedure:

$$\text{Rank to be assigned} = \text{Rank of one score} + \left[\frac{\text{Number of other scores equal to the one score}}{2} \right]$$

Step 1. Start with a rank-group list

To make a rank-group list, the evaluator first wrote 1 next to the highest score, 2 next to the next highest score, and so on, rank ordering the two groups as if they were one group. For tied ranks, he gave the average rank. He called the larger group Group L and the smaller group Group S.

Group L (Program XX)		Group S (Program YY)	
16	12	20	5.5
24	1	14	14.5
18	8.5	18	8.5
23	2	12	16
17	10.5	10	17.5
17	10.5	9	19
14	14.5	22	3
20	5.5	10	17.5
19	7	6	20
21	4		
15	13		

Steps	Example

Step 2. Write down the number in each group

$\boxed{}$ = n_S = Number in smaller group (Group S)

$\boxed{}$ = n_L = Number in larger group (Group L)

Step 3. Going down the rank-group list, record the number of L's which precede each S score

Opposite each S, record the total number of L's above it.

Step 2. Write down the number in each group

n_S = 9 = Number in Group S

n_L = 11 = Number in Group L

Step 3. Going down the rank-group list, record the number of L's which precede each S score

Rank	Group	Number of higher L's
1	L	
2	L	
3	S	2
4	L	
5, 6	LS	3
7	L	
8, 9	LS	5
10, 11	LL	
12	L	
13	L	
14, 15	LS	10
16	S	11
17, 18	SS	11, 11
19	S	11
20	S	11

Step 4. Add up the numbers from Step 3 to find U

$\boxed{}$ = U

Step 5. Calculate U'

$U' = (n_S \times n_L) - U$

$\boxed{}$ = U'

Step 4. Add up the numbers from Step 3 to find U

The total of the numbers in the third column of the table in Step 3 is 75.

$U = \boxed{75}$

Step 5. Calculate U'

$U' = (n_S \times n_L) - U$

$= (9 \times 11) - 75$

$= 99 - 75$

$U' = \boxed{24}$

Steps	Example

Step 6. Record U*

U* (U star) is whichever value, U or U' turns out to be the smaller. Record not only the smaller value but also whether it was U or U'.

```
 _____          _____
|        |  = U* = |        |
|_____|         |_____|
  value             U or U'
```

Step 7. Find the tabled U* value

In the table below, find the column headed by the number in the larger group (n_L). Go down this column until you come to the row for the number in the smaller group (n_S).

Critical Values of U*
For a Two-Tailed Test at a = .10

n_S \ n_L	9	10	11	12	13	14	15	16	17	18	19	20
1											0	0
2	1	1	1	2	2	2	3	3	3	4	4	4
3	3	4	5	5	6	7	7	8	9	9	10	11
4	6	7	8	9	10	11	12	14	15	16	17	18
5	9	11	12	13	15	16	18	19	20	22	23	25
6	12	14	16	17	19	21	23	25	26	28	30	32
7	15	17	19	21	24	26	28	30	33	35	37	39
8	18	20	23	26	28	31	33	36	39	41	44	47
9	21	24	27	30	33	36	39	42	45	48	51	54
10	24	27	31	34	37	41	44	48	51	55	58	62
11	27	31	34	38	42	46	50	54	57	61	65	69
12	30	34	38	42	47	51	55	60	64	68	72	77
13	33	37	42	47	51	56	61	65	70	75	80	84
14	36	41	46	51	56	61	66	71	77	82	87	92
15	39	44	50	55	61	66	72	77	83	88	94	100
16	42	48	54	60	65	71	77	83	89	95	101	107
17	45	51	57	64	70	77	83	89	96	102	109	115
18	48	55	61	68	75	82	88	95	102	109	116	123
19	51	58	65	72	80	87	94	101	109	116	123	130
20	54	62	69	77	84	92	100	107	115	123	130	138

Write this number here:

```
 _____
|        |
|        | = Critical value of U*
|_____|
```

Step 8. Compare the obtained U* value with the tabled U* value

Is the value of U* which you obtained in Step 6 smaller or larger than the tabled U* value from Step 7?

Step 6. Record U*

```
        _____
 U* =  |   24   |  = U'
        ‾‾‾‾‾‾‾‾
```

Step 7. Find the tabled U* value

Since n_S = 9 and n_L = 11, the critical value of U* = 27.

Critical Values of U*
For a Two-Tailed Test at a = .10

n_S \ n_L	9	10	11	12	13	14	15	16	17	18	19	20
1											0	0
2	1	1	1	2	2	2	3	3	3	4	4	4
3	3	4	5	5	6	7	7	8	9	9	10	11
4	6	7	8	9	10	11	12	14	15	16	17	18
5	9	11	12	13	15	16	18	19	20	22	23	25
6	12	14	16	17	19	21	23	25	26	28	30	32
7	15	17	19	21	24	26	28	30	33	35	37	39
8	18	20	23	26	28	31	33	36	39	41	44	47
9	21	24	(27)	30	33	36	39	42	45	48	51	54
10	24	27	31	34	37	41	44	48	51	55	58	62
11	27	31	34	38	42	46	50	54	57	61	65	69
12	30	34	38	42	47	51	55	60	64	68	72	77
13	33	37	42	47	51	56	61	65	70	75	80	84
14	36	41	46	51	56	61	66	71	77	82	87	92
15	39	44	50	55	61	66	72	77	83	88	94	100
16	42	48	54	60	65	71	77	83	89	95	101	107
17	45	51	57	64	70	77	83	89	96	102	109	115
18	48	55	61	68	75	82	88	95	102	109	116	123
19	51	58	65	72	80	87	94	101	109	116	123	130
20	54	62	69	77	84	92	100	107	115	123	130	138

Critical value of U* = | 27 |

Step 8. Compare the obtained U* value with the tabled U* value

Since the obtained value is smaller than the tabled value, one group is significantly higher ranked than the other.

Steps	Example
Step 9. Interpret the statistic	**Step 9. Interpret the statistic**

Step 9. Interpret the statistic

If the obtained U* value was <u>larger</u> than the tabled U* value, then there was no significant difference between the rankings of the two groups.

If the obtained value of U* was <u>smaller</u> than the tabled U*, then there was a statistically significant difference in rankings. To decide which was the higher-ranked group, check back to Step 6:

[.] If U* = U, then the <u>smaller</u> group outranked the larger group

[.] If U* = U', then the <u>larger</u> group outranked the smaller group

Step 9. Interpret the statistic

Group L was the higher ranking group. The evaluator wrote:

"Students from both reading programs participated in a spelling competition. A total of 20 students participated, 11 from Program XX and 9 from Program YY. Two students from Program XX took the first and second places. Third place went to a student from Program YY.

"In order to examine the performance of all the students who entered the competition to see if Program XX students were <u>generally</u> better in spelling, all 20 spelling scores were rank ordered and the Mann-Whitney U Test was applied. The result was statistically significant, indicating that those Program XX students who entered the competition were spelling better than the Program YY students who entered the competition."

Worksheet 3E

The Mann-Whitney U Test:
For Use When There Are More Than
20 Cases in the Larger Group

Steps	Example

Steps

PREVIEW

A statistic, called z, is calculated using the numbers in each group and the number of times one group outranks the other. If z is larger than 1.64, the result is considered statistically significant.

Example

Background

The Chamber of Commerce sponsors a math contest each year at the high school. This year a new trigonometry text had been used in one class, while the old text had been used in the other class. The same teacher taught both classes. The district evaluator decided to use the math contest scores in addition to a district-designed trigonometry test to evaluate the new trigonometry program.

These were the scores from the two groups, Group E and Group C:

Group E		Group C	
Student	Score	Student	Score
AA	90	AV	80
AB	98	AW	94
AC	100	AX	92
AD	100	AY	96
AE	98	AZ	82
AF	80	BA	95
AG	85	BB	86
AH	40	BC	100
AI	99	BD	84
AJ	88	BE	92
AK	50	BF	75
AL	80	BG	95
AM	60	BH	80
AN	96	BI	94
AO	94		
AP	100		
AQ	86		
AR	98		
AS	88		
AT	40		
AU	92		

Steps	Example

Step 1. Rank all the scores, combining both groups

If necessary, see p. 61 for the method of dealing with tied scores.

Step 1. Rank all the scores, combining both groups

In order to rank quickly all the scores, the evaluator made a distribution using a typewriter. (See Worksheet 2B.) She plotted Group E scores with an X, and Group C scores with an O.

Score	Frequency by group	Rank
100	XXXO	2.5
99	X	5
98	XXX	7
96	XO	9.5
95	OO	11.5
94	XOO	14
92	XOO	17
90	X	19
88	XX	20.5
86	XO	22.5
85	X	24
84	O	25
82	O	26
80	XXOO	28.5
75	O	31
60	X	32
50	X	33
40	XX	34.5

Step 2. Record the number in each group

 $= n_S =$ Number in smaller group (Group S)

[ ] $= n_L =$ Number in larger group (Group L)

Step 2. Record the number in each group

$n_S = 14 =$ Number in Group S

$n_L = 21 =$ Number in Group L

Step 3. Add the ranks assigned to the smaller group, Group S

Call the sum R_S.

[ ] $= R_S$

Step 3. Add the ranks assigned to the smaller group, Group S

Ranks assigned to Group S:

$$
\begin{array}{r}
2.5 \\
9.5 \\
11.5 \\
11.5 \\
14 \\
14 \\
17 \\
17 \\
22.5 \\
25 \\
26 \\
28.5 \\
28.5 \\
\underline{31} \\
\end{array}
$$

$R_S = 258.5$

Steps	Example

Step 4. Compute U

$$U = (n_S \cdot n_L) + \frac{n_S (n_S + 1) - R_S}{2}$$

Substeps for computing U:

a. Multiply n_S by $(n_S + 1)$

b. Subtract R_S

c. Divide the result of Substep b by 2 and enter the result here

d. Multiply n_S by n_L

e. Add Substep c and Substep d to obtain U

[ ] = U

Step 5. Compute U'

$$U' = n_S \cdot n_L - U$$

[ ] = U'

Step 6. Record U*

U* (U star) is whichever value, U or U', turns out to be the <u>smaller</u>. Record not only the smaller value, but also whether it was U or U'.

[ ] = U* = [ ]

value   U or U'

Step 4. Compute U

$$U = (n_S \cdot n_L) + \frac{n_S (n_S + 1) - R_S}{2}$$

a. $n_S (n_S + 1) = 14 \cdot 15 =$ [210]

b. $210 - R_S = 210 - 258.5 =$ [-48.5]

c. $\dfrac{-48.5}{2} =$ [-24.25]

d. $n_S \cdot n_L = 14 \cdot 21 =$ [294]

e. $U = 294 + (-24.25) =$ [269.75]

Step 5. Compute U'

$U' = n_S \cdot n_L - U$

    $= 14 \cdot 21 - 269.75$

    $= 294 - 269.75$

$U' =$ [24.25]

Step 6. Record U*

U' was smaller than U.

$U* =$ [24.25] $= U'$

Steps	Example

Steps

Step 7. Substitute U* in this formula

$$z = \frac{U* - \frac{(n_S \cdot n_L)}{2}}{\sqrt{\frac{(n_S \cdot n_L)(n_S + n_L + 1)}{12}}}$$

Steps for computing z:

a. Divide $(n_S \cdot n_L)$, calculated in Step 4d, by 2

b. Subtract this quantity from U*, Step 6

$$\boxed{} = U* - \frac{(n_S \cdot n_L)}{2}$$

c. Add $n_S + n_L + 1$

d. Multiply this quantity by $(n_S \cdot n_L)$, Step 4d

e. Divide the result of Substep d by 12

$$\boxed{} = \frac{(n_S \cdot n_L)(n_S + n_L + 1)}{12}$$

f. Take the square root of the quantity computed in Substep e.

g. Divide Substep b by Substep f to obtain z

$$\boxed{} = z$$

Example

Step 7. Substitute U* in this formula

a.

$$\frac{294}{2} = \boxed{147}$$

b.

$$24.25 - 147 = \boxed{-122.75}$$

c.

$$14 + 21 + 1 = \boxed{36}$$

d.

$$294 \cdot 36 = \boxed{10584}$$

e.

$$\frac{10584}{12} = \boxed{882}$$

f.

$$\sqrt{882} = \boxed{29.7}$$

g.

$$z = \frac{-122.75}{29.7} = \boxed{-4.13}$$

Steps	Example
Step 8. Interpret the statistic	Step 8. Interpret the statistic

Step 8. Interpret the statistic

If the absolute size of z turns out to be larger than 1.64 (ignoring any negative sign z might have), then one set of ranks is significantly higher than the other at the 5% or .05 level.

To decide which was the higher ranked group, check back to Step 6:

· If U* = U, then the _smaller_ group outranked the larger group

· If U* = U', then the _larger_ group outranked the smaller group

Step 8. Interpret the statistic

The statistic z is larger than 1.64 (ignoring the negative sign), so one set of ranks is significantly higher than the other.

Since U* was equal to U', the larger group (Group L) was the group with the significantly higher ranks.

The evaluator concluded that the students using the new trigonometry text did better in the math contest. She would use this information, along with the results of the trigonometry test, to evaluate the effectiveness of the new trigonometry text.

Section II
Comparing Scores From Matched Groups

Use this section when comparing results from two groups, the members of which have been, or can be, *matched*. Since each member of one group is matched with a member of the other group, the numbers in each group will always be the same.

The t-test[13] is a way of testing whether or not two groups can be considered to be equivalent on some measure. The mean score on the measure is computed for each group, and a t-test is used to see if the difference between the two means is large enough to be considered statistically significant or whether the difference is of a size that could easily have occurred by chance.

Suppose you have found that the experimental (E) group's mean was higher than that of the control (C) group. Someone might argue that *any* two groups will generally yield different means when tested. The two groups are not *really* different on the measure; they just appear to be. The observed difference in means is just a reflection of the way sample means always vary. The purpose of the t-test is to see if this argument is correct. The t-test indicates whether the difference in means is greater than would have occurred just because of the only-to-be-expected variation in obtained sample means. If the difference is so large that you would find it fewer than 5 times out of 100 when indeed there was no *real* difference between the E-group and C-group's performance, then it is called statistically significant. Probability of occurrence at this frequency—and more

seldom—has been agreed upon by social scientists to represent a significant finding.

Note, however, that the t-test does not tell you whether or not a statistically significant difference is an *important* difference. You or your evaluation audience will have to judge that for yourselves by examining differences and asking if they are large enough to be considered important educationally.

When To Use the t-test for Matched Groups

Use this test when you need to know if the difference between the results from two *matched* groups is statistically significant, that is, not just a chance result. The pairing, or *matching*, should have been done on the basis of some characteristic likely to be related, positively or negatively, to the outcome measure you are using. Matched groups are discussed more extensively on page 38.

You should also use this test if you wish to see if there have been significant changes in a *single* group between pretest scores and posttest scores. Each student's posttest is matched with his or her own pretest to form the pairs.

---

13. The discussion of the t-test presented on page 41 also applies here. The conceptual basis of the t-test remains the same whether it is performed for matched or unmatched groups; only the calculations change.

Testing the Statistical Significance
of the Difference Between Two Means:
The t-test for Matched Groups

Steps	Example

PREVIEW

You are going to calculate a value called t.

$$t = \frac{(\overline{d})\,(\sqrt{n})}{s_d}$$

This <u>obtained t-value</u> will then be compared with a t-value from a table. If your obtained t-value is <u>larger</u> than the <u>tabled t-value</u>, then the difference between the means is statistically significant.

Background

Thirty students had been formed into 15 matched pairs on the basis of pretest scores. One of each matched pair was assigned to the E-group, the other to the C-group. At the end of the school year, students' scores were as shown in the posttest scores columns of the table in Step 1.

Step 1. Prepare a pair-difference table

Pair	E-group member's score	C-group member's score	Difference in scores
1			
2			
3			
.			
.			
n			

Each difference score is obtained by subtracting the score obtained by one member of the pair from the score obtained by its partner in the pair. It will be best to subtract the C-group score—the score obtained by the member of the pair who is part of the C-group—from the E-group score.

A positive difference is then a difference in favor of the E-group. A negative difference is a difference in favor of the C-group. Usually some differences will be negative and some positive.

Step 1. Prepare a pair-difference table

Pair	Posttest scores		Difference in outcome scores
	E-group	C-group	
1	58.72	56.55	2.17
2	43.05	44.15	-1.10
3	71.00	65.21	5.79
4	52.34	56.34	-4.00
5	49.11	46.91	2.20
6	50.22	48.42	1.80
7	50.46	51.50	-1.04
8	49.03	41.07	7.96
9	42.68	44.02	-1.34
10	78.08	71.00	7.08
11	52.98	53.00	-0.02
12	69.02	70.22	-1.20
13	40.12	36.34	3.78
14	38.04	42.90	-4.86
15	68.04	68.04	0.00

Steps	Example

Step 2. Compute the mean of the set of difference scores

Use Substeps a through d below to calculate the mean of the numbers from the right-hand column in Step 1. This mean of the differences is represented by a d with a line over the top, $\overline{d}$, called "d bar." This figure is also equal to the <u>difference between the first group's mean and the second group's mean</u>. It represents how much better one group did on the average.

Notice that there are positive and negative d's.

a. Add up the positive d's.

       = Sum of positive d's

b. Then add up the negative d's.

       = Sum of negative d's

c. Combine (this means adding a negative number) the results of Substep b and Substep a to obtain the total, or overall, difference.

       = Total d

d. Divide the result of Substep c by the number of pairs. The result is $\overline{d}$.

       = $\overline{d}$

Step 3. Calculate $(\overline{d})\ (\sqrt{n}\ )$

The number of pairs is n. It is the same as the number of d's used in Step 2. Find the <u>square root of n</u>; then multiply that number by $\overline{d}$, computed in Step 2.

       = $(\overline{d})\ (\sqrt{n}\ )$

Step 2. Compute the mean of the set of difference scores

a. Positive d's:

$$
\begin{array}{r}
2.17 \\
5.79 \\
2.20 \\
1.80 \\
7.96 \\
7.08 \\
3.78 \\
\underline{0.00} \\
30.78
\end{array}
$$

b. Negative d's:

$$
\begin{array}{r}
-1.10 \\
-4.00 \\
-1.04 \\
-1.34 \\
-0.02 \\
-1.20 \\
\underline{-4.86} \\
-13.56
\end{array}
$$

c.

$$30.78 + (-13.56)$$

$$30.78 - 13.56 = 17.22 = \text{Total d}$$

d. $\dfrac{17.22}{15} = 1.15$

$\overline{d} = \boxed{1.15}$

Step 3. Calculate $(\overline{d})\ (\sqrt{n}\ )$

n = 15

$\sqrt{n} = \sqrt{15} = 3.87$

$(\overline{d})\ (\sqrt{n}\ ) = (1.15)\ (3.87) = \boxed{4.45}$

Steps

Step 4. Compute the standard deviation of the difference scores

The standard deviation of the difference scores, s_d, read as "s sub d," can be calculated as follows:

a. Add another column to the pair-difference table, and enter the square of each difference, d^2, after each d. To square a number, multiply the number by itself. Find the total of the numbers in this new column.

Pair	d	d^2
1		
2		
3		
n		

Sum d^2 =

b. From the result of Substep a, subtract the <u>square</u> of the result of Step 3. This will leave you with the quantity:

$$\boxed{} = \text{Sum } d^2 - n(\overline{d})^2$$

c. Divide the result of Substep b by n-1. That is, divide by the number that is one less than the number of pairs. The result of this division will be $(s_d)^2$, the variance of the difference scores.

$$\boxed{} = (s_d)^2$$

d. Take the square root of the variance just found in Substep c. This will give you s_d, the standard deviation of the difference scores.

$$\boxed{} = s_d$$

Step 5. Compute the obtained t-value

To do this, divide the result of Step 3 by the final result of Step 4.

$$\boxed{} = \frac{(\overline{d})\ (\sqrt{n}\ )}{s_d} = t$$

Example

Step 4. Compute the standard deviation of the difference scores

a.

Pair	d	d^2
1	2.17	4.71
2	-1.10	1.21
3	5.79	33.52
4	-4.00	16.00
5	2.20	4.84
6	1.80	3.24
7	-1.04	1.08
8	7.96	63.36
9	-1.34	1.80
10	7.08	50.12
11	-0.02	0.00
12	-1.20	1.44
13	3.78	14.29
14	-4.86	23.62
15	0.00	0.00

Sum d^2 = 219.23

b. $219.23 - (4.45)^2$

$219.23 - 19.80 = 199.43$

$\text{Sum } d^2 - n(\overline{d})^2 = 199.43$

c. $\dfrac{199.43}{14} = 14.245$

$(s_d)^2 = 14.245$

d. $\sqrt{14.245} = 3.77$

$s_d = \boxed{3.77}$

Step 5. Compute the obtained t-value

$\dfrac{4.45}{3.77} = 1.18$

$t = \boxed{1.18}$

Steps	Example

Step 6. Select a t-value

It is customary to allow only a 5% chance of wrongly declaring a difference significant. The table below presents t-values based on this 5% chance of error.

Use the t-value in the second column if you predicted, before seeing the results, which group would do better and you were correct.

If you did not predict which group would do better, or if your prediction was incorrect, use the third column to find your tabled t-value.

Tabled t-values

Column 1 Number of pairs	Column 2 If you predicted which group would do better	Column 3 If you didn't predict which group would do better (or were wrong)
7	1.94	2.45
8	1.89	2.36
9	1.86	2.31
10	1.83	2.26
11	1.81	2.23
12	1.80	2.20
13	1.78	2.18
14	1.77	2.16
15	1.76	2.14
16	1.75	2.13
17	1.75	2.12
18	1.74	2.11
19	1.73	2.10
20	1.73	2.09
21	1.72	2.09
22	1.72	2.08
23	1.72	2.07
24	1.71	2.07
25	1.71	2.06
26	1.71	2.06
27	1.71	2.06
28	1.70	2.05
29	1.70	2.05
30	1.70	2.04
31	1.70	2.04
41	1.68	2.02
61	1.67	2.00
121	1.66	1.98
∞*	1.64	1.96

*The infinity sign, ∞, denotes in this case any number greater than 121.

This table is taken from Table III of Fisher and Yates: Statistical Tables for Biological, Agricultural and Medical Research, published by Longman Group Ltd., London (previously published by Oliver and Boyd, Edinburgh), and by permission of the authors and publishers.

Step 6. Select a t-value

It was expected that the E-group students, who had received a new program, would outscore the C-group. That prediction came true, since $\bar{d}$ was positive. Consequently, the evaluator could use a t-value from the second column.

Tabled t-values

Column 1 Number of pairs	Column 2 If you predicted which group would do better	Column 3 If you didn't predict which group would do better (or were wrong)
7	1.94	2.45
8	1.89	2.36
9	1.86	2.31
10	1.83	2.26
11	1.81	2.23
12	1.80	2.20
13	1.78	2.18
14	1.77	2.16
15	(1.76)	2.14
16	1.75	2.13
17	1.75	2.12
18	1.74	2.11
19	1.73	2.10
20	1.73	2.09
21	1.72	2.09
22	1.72	2.08
23	1.72	2.07
24	1.71	2.07
25	1.71	2.06
26	1.71	2.06
27	1.71	2.06
28	1.70	2.05
29	1.70	2.05
30	1.70	2.04
31	1.70	2.04
41	1.68	2.02
61	1.67	2.00
121	1.66	1.98
∞	1.64	1.96

Steps	Example

‖ = tabled t-value

tabled t-value = ‖ 1.76 ‖

Step 7. Compare the obtained t-value with the tabled t-value

Is the obtained t-value as large as the tabled t-value?

Step 8. Interpret the statistic

If the obtained t-value is <u>larger</u> than the tabled t-value, then the difference between the mean scores of the two groups is statistically significant, very unlikely to be just due to chance.

If the obtained t-value is <u>not as large</u> as the tabled t-value, then there is not strong evidence for saying that one group did better than the other group. The difference between mean scores of the E- and C-groups is not statistically significant. It could be just a chance difference.

Examine the educational significance of the result. If the E-group did better than the C-group, <u>how much</u> better? Did the average gain represent valuable extra learning or just a gain of a few items? Making such a judgment is often difficult. Meet with administrators, staff, and possibly community members before you report your results to find out what magnitude of gain they would consider exciting.

Step 7. Compare the obtained t-value with the tabled t-value

The obtained t-value was <u>not</u> as large as the tabled t-value.

Step 8. Interpret the statistic

The t-test showed that the difference between the two groups was not large enough to reach statistical significance. The evaluator had to conclude that as far as <u>these</u> test results showed, the E-group program neither improved scores nor depressed them relative to the control group. In terms of educational significance, both E- and C-group programs appeared to be equally effective.

Calculating the Confidence Limits for the Difference Between Two Means From Matched Groups

Confidence limits[12] are two numbers that estimate the range of differences you would expect to obtain between the mean scores of two groups were you to repeat your study again and again. This gives you an idea of how large a difference you might obtain on occasions other than the present one, with new samples of similar students. Confidence limits also tell you whether your obtained difference is statistically significant by showing whether one of the values you could have found is zero.

After calculating confidence limits, you can say with a certain level of confidence—such as a 5% or 10% chance of being wrong—that the difference will not be smaller than the *lower limit,* the smaller number, or larger than the *upper limit,* the larger number. If you find that the lower confidence limit is zero or below, then you cannot be confident that there will be a difference in favor of the same group if the program were to be repeated. The difference between means is not statistically significant in such a case. Calculating confidence limits, therefore, eliminates the need for a t-test.

When To Use Confidence Limits

When reporting the difference between means, use either a t-test such as the one described by Worksheet 3F to determine statistical significance, *or* use confidence limits. Confidence limits are nearly always preferable, particularly if you plan to discuss the *size* of the difference between the means. Such a discussion will be of interest in program evaluation where your concern is not only *whether* but *how much* difference a program or treatment has made. Confidence limits are generally more easy to explain to lay audiences than are statistics that involve calculating a number foreign to the data at hand, such as a t-value.

Be careful to note, however, that significance as judged by calculating confidence limits does not tell you whether or not your observed difference is an *important* one. You or your evaluation audience will have to judge this for yourselves by asking if it is sufficiently large to be considered important educationally.

---

12. The discussion of confidence limits presented in the Introduction to Worksheet 3B applies here as well. The concepts are the same; only the calculations are different.

Calculating the Confidence Limits for the Difference Between Two Means From Matched Groups

Steps	Example

Steps

Step 1. Prepare a pair-difference list, that is, a list of the difference between each pair of scores

For each pair, record the difference between the outcome measure scores of the two matched members.

Pair	1st member score	2nd member score	Difference in outcome scores, d
1			
2			
3			
.			
.			
n			

Example

Background

Twenty elementary schools in a school district were due to get new reading materials. Two sets of materials were selected by the reading specialist--one set experiential, the other phonics based. The school board was split over the issue of which kind of reading program should be used and asked for both programs to be implemented for a two-year evaluation period.

The evaluator paired the schools according to their average reading achievement scores the year before. He then tossed a coin for each pair of schools to decide which school would receive which program. In this way, ten schools were randomly assigned to an experiential program, and ten _matched_ schools were randomly assigned to phonics, the competing program.

At the end of the first year, all schools took an extensive reading achievement test.

Step 1. Prepare a pair-difference list, that is, a list of the difference between each pair of scores

For each school, the average raw score on the reading test was computed. The schools were grouped in their original pairs, and the following data table was prepared:

School pair	Phonics school mean score	Experiential school mean score	Difference d
1	75.3	70.3	5.0
2	78.2	74.2	4.0
3	69.3	70.0	-0.7
4	70.2	70.1	0.1
5	67.4	67.2	0.2
6	59.8	61.1	-1.3
7	53.5	52.2	1.3
8	48.0	42.8	5.2
9	48.4	42.0	6.4
10	45.0	45.2	-0.2
	615.1	595.1	

Steps	Example

Step 2. Compute the mean of the set of difference scores

Use Substeps a through d below to calculate the mean of the numbers from the right-hand column in Step 1. This mean of the differences is represented by a d with a line over the top, $\overline{d}$, called "d bar." This figure is also equal to the <u>difference between the first group's mean and the second group's mean</u>. It represents how much better one group did on the average.

Notice that there are positive and negative d's.

a. Add up the positive d's.

   = Sum of positive d's

b. Then add up the negative d's.

[   ]   = Sum of negative d's

c. Combine (this means adding a negative number) the results of Substep b and Substep a to obtain the total, or overall, difference.

[   ]   = Total d

d. Divide the result of Substep c by the number of pairs. The result is $\overline{d}$.

[   ]   = $\overline{d}$

Step 3. Compute the standard deviation of the difference scores

The standard deviation of the difference scores, s_d, read as "s sub d," can be calculated as follows:

a. Add another column to the pair-difference table, and enter the square of each difference, d^2, after each d. To square a number, multiply the number by itself. Find the total of the numbers in this new column.

Pair	d	d^2
1		
2		
3		
.		
.		

Sum d^2 =

Step 2. Compute the mean of the set of difference scores

a. Positive d's:
	5.0
	4.0
	0.1
	0.2
	1.3
	5.2
	6.4
	22.2

b. Negative d's:
	−0.7
	−1.3
	−0.2
	−2.2

c.

22.2 + (−2.2)

22.2 − 2.2 = 20.0 = Total d

d. $\dfrac{20.0}{10}$ = 2.00 = Mean d

$\overline{d}$ = 2.00

Step 3. Compute the standard deviation of the difference scores

a.

Pair	d	d^2
1	5.0	25.00
2	4.0	16.00
3	−0.7	.49
4	0.1	.01
5	0.2	.04
6	−1.3	1.69
7	1.3	1.69
8	5.2	27.04
9	6.4	40.96
10	−0.2	.04

Sum d^2 = 112.96

Steps	Example

b. Compute the quantity $n(\overline{d})^2$. To do this, take the result of Step 2, square it, and then multiply by n, the number of pairs.

$$\boxed{} = n(\overline{d})^2$$

b. $10 \ (2)^2 = 10 \cdot 4 = 40$

$$n(\overline{d})^2 = 40$$

c. From the result of Substep a, subtract the result of Substep b. This will leave you with the quantity:

$$\boxed{} = \text{Sum } d^2 - n(\overline{d})^2$$

c. $112.96 - 40 = 72.96$

$$\text{Sum } d^2 - n(\overline{d})^2 = 72.96$$

d. Divide the result of Substep c by n-1. That is, divide by the number that is one less than the number of pairs. The result of this division will be $(s_d)^2$, the variance of the difference scores.

$$\boxed{} = (s_d)^2$$

d. $\dfrac{72.96}{9} = 8.1$

$$(s_d)^2 = 8.1$$

e. Take the square root of the variance just found in Substep d. This will give you s_d, the standard deviation of the difference scores.

$$\boxed{} = s_d$$

e. $\sqrt{8.1} = 2.85$

$$s_d = \boxed{2.85}$$

Step 4. Choose a t-value

Now you need a number called t. This value depends upon how many <u>scores</u> were in each group and on how <u>sure</u> you want to be of the confidence limits.

Choose your t-value from the table on the following page. Go down the first column to locate the row which starts with the number of matched pairs that you are working with. Then choose one of the t-values on that row.

To decide if you want to use the t-value from the second or third column, decide how strict you want to be about the confidence limits. Do you want 95% confidence about the upper and lower boundaries of differences? That is, do you want the confidence limits to define a range into which 95 out of any 100 differences you would calculate would fall?

If you choose the 95% limits, you will be <u>very</u> sure of including the true difference* between the mean of the first group and the mean of the second group, but these limits will be further apart and

*The true difference is the average result you would obtain over many trials of the same kind.

Step 4. Choose a t-value

The evaluator decided that in view of this being the first year, it was important to catch any possible advantage of one program over another. He was more interested in a trend than a final decision. He therefore selected the 80% column.

	Steps			Example	

therefore more likely to include zero in their range, indicating a lack of statistical significance.

By choosing this strict 95% column, you reduce the chance of your saying there was a significant difference when there was only a by-chance difference. On the other hand, you increase the chance of making another error--the error of declaring no significant difference when there was a difference, but one obscured by the score variability within each group. Try to decide which kind of error would be worse, and choose a column accordingly.

Number of pairs	4 out of 5 odds (80% confidence)	95 out of 100 odds (95% confidence)
7	1.44	2.45
8	1.41	2.36
9	1.40	2.31
10	1.38	2.26
11	1.37	2.23
12	1.36	2.20
13	1.36	2.18
14	1.35	2.16
15	1.35	2.14
16	1.34	2.13
17	1.34	2.12
18	1.33	2.11
19	1.33	2.10
20	1.33	2.09
21	1.32	2.09
22	1.32	2.08
23	1.32	2.07
24	1.32	2.07
25	1.32	2.06
26	1.32	2.06
31	1.31	2.04
41	1.30	2.02
61	1.30	2.00
121	1.29	1.98
∞*	1.28	1.96

*The infinity sign, ∞, denotes in this case any number greater than 121.

The third column, the .05 level, represents the conventional minimal level of certainty demanded by the social sciences. Some evaluation theorists have argued that it is too demanding for the large scale studies conducted by evaluators. In your situation, therefore, if a chance of being right four out of five times is good enough, then choose the 80% level. If your data, however, stand up under the 95% test, then by all means use it.

Record your choice here:

[ ] = t-value

Example

Number of pairs	4 out of 5 odds (80% confidence)	95 out of 100 odds (95% confidence)
7	1.44	2.45
8	1.41	2.36
9	1.40	2.31
10	(1.38)	2.26
11	1.37	2.23
12	1.36	2.20
13	1.36	2.18
14	1.35	2.16
15	1.35	2.14
16	1.34	2.13
17	1.34	2.12
18	1.33	2.11
19	1.33	2.10
20	1.33	2.09
21	1.32	2.09
22	1.32	2.08
23	1.32	2.07
24	1.32	2.07
25	1.32	2.06
26	1.32	2.06
31	1.31	2.04
41	1.30	2.02
61	1.30	2.00
121	1.29	1.98
∞	1.28	1.96

t-value = [1.38]

Steps	Example

Step 5. Compute the confidence limits

$$\text{Upper limit} = \overline{d} + \frac{(t \cdot s_d)}{\sqrt{n}} \qquad \text{Lower limit} = \overline{d} - \frac{(t \cdot s_d)}{\sqrt{n}}$$

a. Compute and write down $\sqrt{n}$, the square root of the number of matched pairs.

$$\boxed{} = \sqrt{n}$$

b. You have t from Step 4 and s_d from Step 3. Multiply these numbers and divide by $\sqrt{n}$, the number from Substep a.

$$\boxed{} = \frac{t \cdot s_d}{\sqrt{n}}$$

c. To compute the <u>upper</u> confidence limit, <u>add</u> the result of Substep b to $\overline{d}$, the quantity computed in Step 2.

$$\boxed{} = \overline{d} + \frac{(t \cdot s_d)}{\sqrt{n}}$$

d. To compute the <u>lower</u> confidence limit, <u>subtract</u> the quantity in Substep b from $\overline{d}$.

$$\boxed{} = \overline{d} - \frac{(t \cdot s_d)}{\sqrt{n}}$$

Step 6. Interpret the statistic

<u>Does the confidence interval--that is, the range of values from the lower limit to the upper limit --include zero?</u> IF YES, the obtained difference between means could have been due to chance. The difference between the groups is not statistically significant.

IF NO, if both limits are positive or both are negative, then you can state with a certain amount of confidence--the odds you chose in selecting a t-value--that the difference between means could be expected to occur again in favor of the same group if the program were repeated. The obtained difference is statistically significant, not just due to chance. What this means is that there is a high probability that the same group would come out ahead if the same kind of study were performed again. You may want to say that a chance difference as large as the obtained d would be likely, having a probability of less than 20% if you chose the 80% column, or a probability of less than 5% if you chose the 95% column.

Step 5. Compute the confidence limits

a. $\sqrt{n} = \sqrt{10}$

  $\sqrt{n} = 3.16$

b. $\dfrac{t \cdot s_d}{\sqrt{n}} = \dfrac{(1.38)\,(2.85)}{3.16}$

  $\dfrac{t \cdot s_d}{\sqrt{n}} = 1.24$

c.

  $2.00 + 1.24 = \boxed{3.24} = \text{upper limit}$

d.

  $2.00 - 1.24 = \boxed{0.76} = \text{lower limit}$

Step 6. Interpret the statistic

This is how the evaluator reported the results:

"The average reading test raw score for those schools using the phonics program was 61.51. For the matched group of schools using the experimental program, the mean score was 59.51 These results are displayed in Figure A.

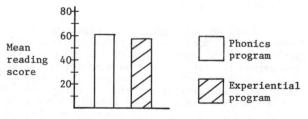

<u>Figure A.</u> Mean reading scores of the phonics and experiential reading programs

Steps	Example
<u>What is the educational significance of the results?</u> If your answer to the above question was no, you now know the result was statistically significant. Next you need to examine the educational significance of the result. Note the value of $\overline{d}$, the average difference between the E-group scores and their matched pairs. The difference represents your best guess about the average effect that can be expected on repeating the program. The importance of this difference needs to be carefully considered by the evaluator and others concerned. Is it an important average difference, representing fairly impressive gains? Or is it, considering the expense and time involved in producing the difference, rather disappointingly small? If it is small, does it nevertheless represent a promising start, likely to be improved upon by running the program longer? Confidence limits help you in these deliberations by revealing how great a difference you could expect from repeated studies of the same kind. Consider the lower confidence limit. Suppose it represents the true extent of the difference between the groups. Would you then conclude that one of the groups had a substantial educational advantage over the other? Now consider the upper confidence limit. Would you draw the same conclusion with respect to educational advantage? If you reach the same conclusion whether the upper or lower confidence limit is taken as the true difference between the groups, then the results of your study have provided you with a clear message. That message may point to one program's superiority or to a "tie score." On the other hand, if the upper confidence limit leads to one conclusion, and the lower confidence limit leads to the opposite conclusion, then you have <u>no</u> firm basis for decision-making.	"The difference of 2.00 points in favor of the phonics program schools represents a statistically significant result. Repetitions of the program could be expected to produce differences somewhere between 0.76 and 3.24 points in favor of the phonics program. "Even though the phonics program students scored significantly better, the difference reflected in the confidence limits ranges from a 1-point advantage to about a 3-point advantage for phonics; in either case, the difference is nothing to get excited about. "I suggest that we consider the educational impact of the two programs to be about equal. Let's see how students in the two programs perform at the end of <u>next</u> year. If the difference in achievement scores is still small, then we'll base our choice of program on cost and other factors."

Introduction to Worksheet 3H
Comparing Two Groups if the Outcome Measures Are Comparisons Rather Than Scores: The Sign Test

Suppose the experimental E-group and the control or competing C-group were formed by first matching students, teachers, classrooms, or schools on some characteristic and then assigning them randomly to either the experimental or control group. At the end of the program, the matched cases are examined to see whether the scores from the E-group tend to exceed their matched partners who had been in the C-group. In this case, the *sign test* provides a very simple, easily computed test of the significance of the differences between two groups of matched pairs when these differences are based on simple comparisons between each pair. A *simple comparison* is one that says which member of the pair is higher on some dimension. For example, one student in each pair might be *judged* to be more assertive, or to have a more positive attitude toward school. A simple comparison makes no effort to say *how much* more assertive, or *how much* more positive; only the *direction* of the comparison is recorded. The sign test examines all the comparisons between the members of two groups and decides whether the number of comparisons in favor of one group is significantly higher than the number in favor of the other. An excess of comparisons in favor of the E-group indicates that the group has indeed been affected by the program.

When To Use the Sign Test

Use the sign test when your situation matches one of the following:

1. Students in the E- and C-groups are or can be matched on some relevant pre-program characteristic(s), something likely to be related to the expected outcome.
2. The outcome measure is a comparison rather than a score. For example, the outcome measure is a judgment of higher or lower, but not of *how much* higher or lower. The sign test is particularly useful with measures which only allow a *qualitative* judgment such as an observer's opinion about some feature of the program implementation, or teachers' ratings of the relative quality of term papers.

When interpreting results from the sign test, be careful to note that the test does not tell you whether or not the significant difference you have found is an *important* one. Because the data that feed into the sign test consist of simple comparisons, you should not use result of this test as your sole basis for making important decisions.

Comparing Two Groups if the Outcome Measures Are Comparisons Rather Than Scores: The Sign Test

Steps	Example

PREVIEW

You will calculate a number which indicates how probable your particular results would be if the comparisons made between the pairs had been random.

If it turns out that the result was highly improbable, then this indicates a statistically significant result rather than simply the effects of chance variation.

Background

An in-service course on "Creating a Learning Environment" was being offered in a district during April and had to be evaluated. Principals were asked to nominate pairs of teachers whose rooms were of about the same "visual quality." One of each pair was randomly offered the in-service course. Five weeks after the course finished, the district office in-service director visited the classrooms of each pair of the originally nominated teachers. After visiting a pair of classrooms, he noted which had the better visual quality. He was not informed which classroom of each pair belonged to a teacher who had received the in-service training.

Step 1. Prepare a list of pairs and their outcome results

Start with a list of the pairs of cases which were originally matched and are now to be compared. Each pair consists of an E-group member and a C-group member.

Record the result of the outcome comparison in this way: Write down a "+" if the E-group member exceeded the C-group member. Record a "-" if the C-group member was higher. The "+" indicates that a comparison is in favor of the E-group; the "-" indicates a comparison the other way. If the pair comparison showed no difference, record a zero.

Step 1. Prepare a list of pairs and their outcome results

Pair number	Judgment of visual quality
1	+
2	+
3	0
4	+
5	0
6	–
7	–
8	0
9	–
10	+
11	–
12	+
13	0
14	–
15	0
16	0
17	0
18	+
19	+
20	+

Key:

+ classroom of teacher who has had the in-service course was judged superior in visual quality to that of teacher who had not had the course

– teacher who has had no in-service course was judged superior

0 unable to judge one classroom superior to other

Steps	Example

Step 2. Prune the list

Eliminate any pairs in which there was no discernible difference on the posttest.

Step 2. Prune the list

Pair number	Judgment of visual quality
1	+
2	+
~~3~~	~~0~~
4	+
~~5~~	~~0~~
6	−
7	−
~~8~~	~~0~~
9	−
10	+
11	−
12	+
~~13~~	~~0~~
14	−
~~15~~	~~0~~
~~16~~	~~0~~
~~17~~	~~0~~
18	+
19	+
20	+

Step 3. Find x

a. Count the number of "+"s and the number of "−"s, and record these here:

[ ] = number of "+"s

[ ] = number of "−"s

b. Compute the sum, which is the number of pairs to be used in the analysis.

[ ] = n

c. Determine which is smaller--the number of "+"s or the number of "−"s. Let the <u>smaller number</u> be x, and write it down.

[ ] = x

Step 3. Find x

a.

Number of "+"s = 8

Number of "−"s = 5

b.

n = 13

c.

x = 5

Steps	Example

Step 4. Test the significance of the result

If you have 25 or fewer pairs, use the table below. Go down column (n) until you locate the number of pairs to be used in your analysis. If x is equal to or smaller than the corresponding number in the second column, then there is a statistically significant result. If x is larger than the appropriate number in the second column, a statistically significant result has not been established.

Step 4. Test the significance of the result

The value read from the table for 13 pairs was 3. Since the value of x was 5, which is larger than 3, a statistically significant result had not been established. It could not be said that the results of the in-service were clear to a visitor.

Table for the Sign Test
When There Are Fewer Than 26 Pairs

Number of pairs used in analysis (n)	Value that x must not exceed for significance at 10%
5	0
6	0
7	0
8	1
9	1
10	2
11	2
12	2
13	3
14	3
15	3
16	4
17	4
18	5
19	5
20	5
21	6
22	6
23	7
24	7
25	8

Number of pairs used in analysis (n)	Value that x must not exceed for significance at 10%
5	0
6	0
7	0
8	1
9	1
10	2
11	2
12	2
13	3
14	3
15	3
16	4
17	4
18	5
19	5
20	5
21	6
22	6
23	7
24	7
25	8

If you have more than 25 pairs, compute z using this formula:

$$z = \frac{n - (2x + 1)}{\sqrt{n}}$$

The next September, however, the course was offered again to a larger number of randomly selected teachers from pairs nominated by principals. The computations were as follows:

Number of "+"s = 28

Number of "−"s = 11

n = 39

x = 11

Substeps for computing z:

a. Double x

a.

	= 2x

2x = 22

Steps	Example

b. Add one

$$\boxed{} \;=\; 2x + 1$$

c. Subtract the result of Substep b from n, the number of pairs

$$\boxed{} \;=\; n - (2x + 1)$$

d. Compute $\sqrt{n}$

$$\boxed{} \;=\; \sqrt{n}$$

e. Divide Substep c by Substep d to obtain z

$$\boxed{} \;=\; \frac{n - (2x + 1)}{\sqrt{n}} \;=\; z$$

If z is <u>equal to or larger</u> than 1.64, you have a statistically significant result at the 5% or .05 level.

---

b.

$$2x + 1 = 23$$

c.

$$n - (2x + 1) = 39 - 23 = 16$$

d.

$$\sqrt{n} = \sqrt{39} = 6.24$$

e.

$$z = \frac{16}{6.24} = \boxed{2.56}$$

The z value of 2.56 is <u>larger</u> than 1.64. This time, therefore, the result was statistically significant. The in-service course seemed to have improved the appearance of teachers' rooms.

The evaluator suggested that the positive results the second time might have been due to the fact that the in-service course was given at a time when teachers were more likely to work on their rooms--September rather than April.

Chapter 4

Examining Relationships Between Two Measures Made on the Same Group

Was reading achievement related to the amount of time spent in the remedial reading laboratory?

Is a child's achievement rank in his own classroom related to his self-esteem score?

Is a teacher's experience in terms of number of years spent teaching related to the percentage of his students who subsequently enroll in college?

This part of the book deals with these kinds of questions: detecting the *relationship* between two measures.

The most commonly used measure of relationship is the correlation coefficient, usually denoted by *r*. Several kinds of correlation coefficient are available to you. Your choice will be determined by the characteristics of your measures. The most widely used coefficient is Pearson's Product Moment Coefficient, Worksheet 4B. Most other correlation coefficients are also basically Pearson's Product Moment Coefficients, calculated by formulas which have been modified because of the kinds of scores with which they deal. These other correlation coefficients, which are presented here on separate worksheets, are Phi Coefficient, Point Biserial Correlation Coefficient, and Spearman's Rank Order Correlation Coefficient. Spearman's Rank Order Correlation Coefficient is applicable to a large variety of measures and is simple to calculate. It is presented on Worksheet 4C. This section also contains a discussion of the Chi-square test (Worksheet 4H) for detecting significant relationships.

The Meaning of the Correlation Coefficient, r

The correlation between two measures is always expressed as a decimal number between −1 and +1. It indicates whether there is a simple relationship between two measures. If high scores on one measure tend to be obtained by the same students who obtained high scores on the other measure, and likewise low scores are associated with low scores, then there is a *positive* correlation between the two measures. For example, achievement is usually higher for students whose IQ scores are higher: there is a positive relationship between achievement measures and IQ measures. If every student's achievement score were an *exact* reflection of his IQ score, then the correlation between achievement and IQ would be r=1.00. The graph for a correlation of 1.00, a perfect correlation, would be a set of points like those in Figure 3. A straight line could be drawn through them as in Figure 4.

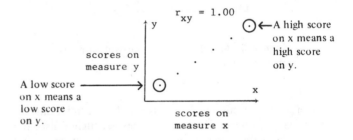

Figure 3. Scores from two measures having a perfect positive correlation

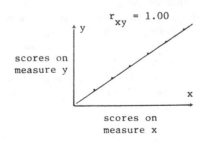

Figure 4. Graph of scores showing a perfect positive correlation

However, since no measures are perfect and since IQ is only one of many influences on achievement, the correlation between ability and achievement measures is usually only about r = 0.60, considerably less than a *perfect* 1.00, but still a fairly strong relationship. A correlation of 0.60 looks something like Figure 5 below. The points lie more or less *around* a straight line. A line can be drawn in to show the trend, as in Figure 6.

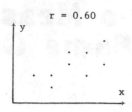

Figure 5. Scores from two measures showing a positive correlation of .60

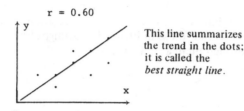

Figure 6. Graph of scores showing a positive correlation of .60

So far this discussion has illustrated only relationships where, as x scores get higher, y scores get higher also, the case in which there is a *positive* correlation between x and y. If, however, one variable gets *smaller* as the other gets *bigger,* then there is a *negative* correlation. For example, it might be the case that the percentage of parents participating in school activities decreases with increasing school size; that is, *smaller* schools show a *larger* percentage of parents participating in school activities than do larger schools. If you collected school size and parent participation data from a large number of schools and computed the correlation coefficient, it might be r = -0.30, a weak and *negative* relationship. The graph of a negative correlation slopes downward rather than upward, as shown in Figure 7, a hypothetical example.

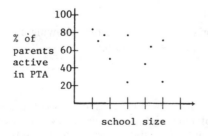

Figure 7. Scores showing a negative correlation of -.30

When Not To Use r

It is important to note that the correlation coefficient is only completely satisfactory as an indicator of relationships if the relationships are more or less *linear,* that is, if a graph of the data shows a straight line rather than a curved one.

For example, it may be that *moderately anxious* persons do better on tests than persons who are so lacking in anxiety that they don't really wake up and try. This suggests a *positive* correlation between achievement and anxiety—*higher* anxiety associated with *higher* achievement. But if people are *very highly* anxious rather than just moderately anxious, they may make mistakes and thus lower their achievement. In this case, *higher* anxiety may then become associated with *lower* achievement—a *negative* correlation. Figure 8 shows the postulated situation.

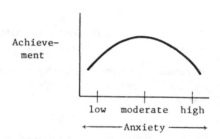

Figure 8. Hypothetical relationship between anxiety and achievement

Here, *use of the correlation coefficient would be inappropriate* since the graph is not a straight line. Calculation of r would yield a very low, non-significant value even though there was a strong but *curvilinear* relationship.

The size of the correlation coefficient shows how well a *straight line* fits the data when the two measures are plotted on a graph. To make sure that fitting a straight line is appropriate for your data, *graph the data before calculating r.* This important process is illustrated in Worksheet 4A. If, when you plot the data, you discover a curved relationship, use the Chi-square test (Worksheet 4H) as your measure of relationship, translating your measures into categories.

How To Choose the Proper Correlation Coefficient

There are several kinds of correlation coefficients:

Method of Calculating r	Symbol
Phi (read phēē) Coefficient	ϕ
Rank Biserial Correlation Coefficient	r_{rb}
Point Biserial Correlation Coefficient	r_{pb}
Spearman's Rank Order Correlation Coefficient	r_s
Pearson's Product Moment Correlation Coefficient	r or r_{xy}

Choosing which you should use is a matter of deciding what kinds of measures you are dealing with. The word *measure* is used loosely here to mean any activity—even rummaging through cumulative record files—that assigns a person (or class, or whatever) to a category or score.

First, think about the *kind of conclusion* each measure produces. *What happens to a person being measured?* Is she classified, ranked, rated? Does she receive a score? Focus on the outcome of the *whole* measure, not *individual items,* since a single measure can contain several different types of items.

Then ask yourself this question: *Is the result of one of the measures placement of cases into categories which have names but no particular order?* Table 1 shows examples of such *nominal* measures.

TABLE 1

Examples of Nominal Measures Which Place Cases Into Categories With No Particular Order

Measure	Categories
Ethnicity	Afro, Asian, Caucasian, Spanish, Indian
Type of reading program	Apple Valley, Universal Reading System
School attended	Roosevelt, Lincoln, Washington
Area of USA	Northwest, Pacific Coast, New England
Home ownership	Yes, No

IF YES, ask yourself another question:

Does the measure place cases into only *two* categories?

- *IF YES*, you have a *dichotomous measure,* and you can calculate one of the three correlation coefficients listed in Table 2 in the column labeled "Dichotomous."

- *IF NO,* that is, if the nominal measure places cases into more than two categories, then no correlation coefficient can be calculated. However, you might be able to perform a Chi-square test, page 122 and Worksheet 4H. Chi-square tells you whether there is a statistically significant relationship between the two measures. Before you can do a Chi-square test, the results of both measures must be in the form of categories. Chi-square does *not* produce a correlation coefficient. It will not tell you *how much* relationship there seems to be between two measures, only whether or not there seems to be one at all.

TABLE 2

Appropriate Correlation Coefficients for Use With Dichotomous, Ordinal, or Interval Measures

Classification of FIRST MEASURE	Classification of SECOND MEASURE		
	Dichotomous	Ordinal	Interval
Dichotomous **Examples** • Yes - No • Agree - Disagree • U.S. Citizen - Alien • Preschool - No preschool • Like - Dislike	Phi Coefficient ϕ	rank biserial r_{rb}	point biserial r_{pb}
Ordinal **Examples** • Rank in class • Low, moderate, high • Never, sometimes, often • Negative, neutral, positive	rank biserial r_{rb}	Spearman's rank order r_s	Spearman's rank order r_s
Interval **Examples** • Arithmetic score • Reading achievement • IQ	Point biserial r_{pb}	Spearman's rank order r_s	Pearson's product moment[14] r_{xy}

IF NO, refer to Table 2 to choose an appropriate correlation coefficient, but first classify your measure as *ordinal* or *interval:*

- *Ordinal measures* result in two or more values which arrange people in some kind of *order.* The order represents an increase in something, say achievement or positive attitude, which is expected to be related to a change in some other measure.

  Ordinal data, while placing people in order, do not, however, tell you *how far apart* they are. A person's falling into a middle category, for instance, does not mean that she is equally distant from the adjacent categories above and below. For example, if

14. If the distribution of scores from either of the two measures is highly skewed, bimodal, or otherwise far from normal, it is advisable to use r_s rather than r_{xy}. Since r_s is quicker and simpler to calculate, you may wish to use it anyway to save time and effort. The price you pay will be a lower value than r_{xy}, but still a good indication of correlation.

the frequency of use of materials is reported in terms of *never, rarely, sometimes, frequently,* and *always,* no assumption is made that the difference between rarely and sometimes is the same size as the difference between frequently and always. Another example of an ordinal scale is *low, moderate,* and *high,* which might be used to measure, say, anxiety. A commonly used ordinal scale is rank in class.

- *Interval measures* have a set of values along a scale made up of equal intervals. That is, the difference between any two adjacent values is assumed to be equal to the difference between any other two adjacent values. This is the case with measures of the *amount* of something respondents possess. Achievement tests are usually considered to be interval measures.

To select an appropriate correlation coefficient, decide whether your first measure is dichotomous, ordinal, or interval. Then decide the same thing for your second measure. Finally, locate the appropriate cell in Table 2. It makes no difference which measure you label first or second.

Having selected the appropriate correlation coefficient, find its worksheet:

Correlation Coefficient	Worksheet
Pearson's Product Moment, r	4B
Spearman's Rank Order, r_s	4C
Phi Coefficient, $\emptyset$	4D
Rank Biserial, r_{rb}	4E
Point Biserial, r_{pb}	4F

After you have calculated the correlation coefficient, you will still need to check whether it is *statistically significant.* To test for significance, it is recommended that you compute confidence limits using Worksheet 4G.

Interpreting Correlation Coefficients

This section discusses how to determine how much confidence to place in a particular correlation coefficient. The recommended approach is to establish *confidence limits* around the coefficient. These limits show how large or small a correlation you might have gotten were you to administer the measures and correlate them again. They also tell you whether or not the correlation you have obtained is significantly different from a correlation of zero.

Figure 9 provides a rough guide to interpreting the size of r:

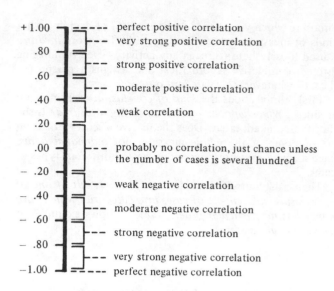

Figure 9. The range of possible correlations and their usual interpretations

A strong correlation means a close relationship between the two measures. As one measure takes on different values, you will find that the values of the other measure will change consistently also. Thus if you have a strong correlation between an ability and an achievement measure, and you pick out cases of high ability, the achievement scores of these cases will tend to be high too. When there is a strong correlation, you can use that correlation *to predict a score on one measure from knowledge of a score on the other measure.*

Confidence Limits for r

Once you have computed a correlation coefficient, say r = 0.60, you still need to know how stable this value is likely to be. The question boils down to this: *If you selected a different sample of cases from which to compute r, would you be likely to get r = 0.60 again or a value quite different?* Confidence limits, whose calculation is directed by Worksheet 4G, give you upper and lower boundaries for values you might expect to get.

If you had computed r = 0.60 from a sample of *25 cases,* for example, the confidence limits would be about 0.27 (lower limit) to 0.80 (upper limit), as shown in Figure 10. These limits are based on use of a 0.05 significance level—that is, a 5% chance that the actual correlation coefficient lies outside the range which they define.

A confidence limit range from .27 to .80 means that with other *samples* of size 25 you might get values in the range from .27 to .80. *You can see why the correlation coefficient has been called a slippery statistic; it is likely to be very variable.* However, the larger the number of cases, the less slippery will be the correlation coefficient. For example, Figure 11 shows the confidence limits that would surround r = .60 were they to be calculated from 200 cases.

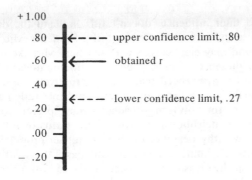

Figure 10. Confidence limits around r = .60 for 25 cases

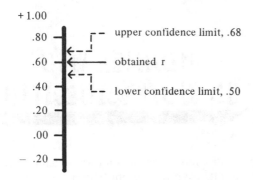

Figure 11. Confidence limits around r = .60 for 200 cases at 0.05 confidence level

This shows that with other samples of 200, you might get values that range from .50 to .68. These values are not much different from the obtained value of .60. The large number of cases allows you to place great confidence in the representativeness of the obtained correlation.

If *zero* is included within the range of the confidence limits around r, this means that you might find a zero correlation when working with similar samples using the same measures. In such a case, you must report that the correlation is *not statistically significant.* Figure 12 shows an example:

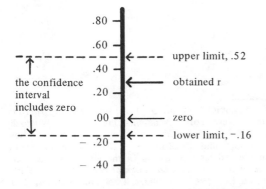

Figure 12. Confidence limits around r = .30 for 20 cases

Since the confidence interval includes the zero point, the obtained correlation of r = .30 is not significantly different from zero. *You cannot claim that there is a significant correlation in such a case.*

Upper and lower confidence limits can be found by reading the chart in Figure 14, page 116 according to the directions in Worksheet 4G. Actually, Figure 14 should only be used for Pearson's Product Moment Correlation Coefficient. If you use it with other coefficients, think of your results as a general indication of the stability of the coefficient, and consult a statistics text[15] for more exact limits.

Now suppose that, using Worksheet 4G, you find a correlation that is not significantly different from zero—the confidence limits span zero—and you had strongly expected that there *would* be a significant correlation. Then one or more of the following situations may have occurred:

1. You were wrong—there really is *no* relationship.
2. You were correct, but you measured too few cases to get an accurate measure of the correlation. A sample size of 30 or larger is advisable when dealing with correlations.
3. You were correct, but the relationship is *curvilinear* rather than *linear*.
4. You were correct, but one or both of your measures did not produce sufficient *score variability* to allow the correlation to show up.

Imagine, for example, that you want to correlate the scores from a mathematics achievement test given to high school seniors with an index of participation in school athletics, but math scores are available only for the district's gifted students. Whatever correlation coefficient you obtain, it will probably be *lower* than the actual correlation because you have restricted the range of one measure's scores, as illustrated in Figure 13.

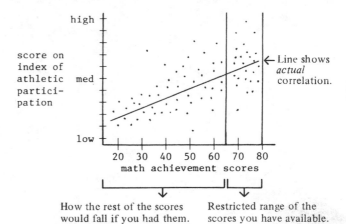

How the rest of the scores would fall if you had them.   Restricted range of the scores you have available.

Figure 13. Illustration of how restricting the range of scores on one measure decreases the chance of obtaining a significant correlation. Only a view of the full range of math scores would show the relationship.

15. For instance, Glass, G. V., & Stanley, J. C. *Statistical methods in education and psychology.* Englewood Cliffs, NJ: Prentice Hall, 1970.

The figure shows that in reality there is a modest but definitely positive correlation between math achievement score and athletic participation. Since you are able to examine only a narrow band of scores, with considerable variability on the athletic index, however, the correlation is not apparent.

Problems 3 and 4 can best be dealt with through consultation with a data analyst.

A Word of Caution You Have Probably Heard Before

Be careful to avoid a trap into which many researchers and evaluators have fallen: *Remember that establishing the existence of a relationship between two measures does not tell you what has caused it.* If, for instance, it has been shown that students who spend more time in the reading lab have higher reading achievement scores, what interpretation can be made? Was the reading lab improving reading, or were better-reading students choosing to spend more time in the reading lab or being sent to the reading lab more often by teachers? In general, if there is a relationship between X and Y, this does not tell us whether X causes Y, or Y causes X. And frequently it could be the case that *neither* inference about causes is correct: other factors may cause both X and Y.

To illustrate, suppose a high positive correlation has been found between length of teachers' experience in a school and percent of students going on to college. It might be thought that the relationship indicates that more experienced teachers are more effective at preparing students for college. Since going to college occurs after teachers have had their influence, doesn't this indicate the direction of cause-and-effect? Not necessarily. Students who are college bound may elect classes with teachers who like to teach. So the presence of college bound students might cause retention of experienced teachers. Alternatively—or maybe additionally, since there are usually multiple rather than single causes for anything—teachers may prefer to teach in wealthy neighborhoods for salary, status or other reasons, and wealthy neighborhoods have higher proportions of students attending college. In this case, the relationship between the measures may occur because both are related to a third measure—neighborhood wealth.

The caution that finding a relationship does not establish causality has been so often repeated that it might as well be engraved in stone.

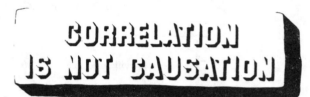

This is, of course, a good thing to remember when dealing with results from only a single study. But an *accumulation* of correlational evidence can, in some instances, help you to build a credible case for a causal relationship between two characteristics. Quite a bit of recent and excellent work in statistics has focused on this complex issue.[16]

---

16. See, for example: Duncan, O. D. *Introduction to structural equation models.* New York: Academic Press, 1975. Wittrock, M. C., & Wiley, D. E. (Eds.). *The evaluation of instruction.* New York: Holt, Rinehart and Winston, 1970 (Particularly useful are Chapter 1 and the articles reproduced in the appendix). Blalock, H. M. *Causal inferences in nonexperimental research.* New York: W. W. Norton and Co., 1961. Kerlinger, F. N. and Pedhazur, E. J. *Multiple regression in behavioral research.* New York: Holt, Rinehart and Winston, 1973 (Particularly the section on path analysis in Chapter 11.).

Steps	Example

Background

The coordinator of a bilingual education program was trying to locate the classrooms which had been most successful in raising the English reading achievement of bilingual children. Raven's Standard Progressive Matrices (SPM) had been used as a pretest. Since the test contained no words or numbers, the coordinator wondered if it really would correlate with posttest scores on an English reading test. If it did, she would take this pretest into account when examining posttest scores.

Before plotting data from many classrooms, she took the scores from one bilingual classroom to plot as a sample. These scores were displayed in the following table.

Student	Pretest (SPM)	Posttest (reading)
A	40	80
B	35	60
C	38	67
D	42	70
E	49	83
F	20	50
G	36	67
H	42	70
I	31	55
J	21	48
K	39	67
L	45	78
M	27	56
N	39	70
O	24	50
P	12	55
Q	18	40
R	32	65
S	36	62
T	31	55
U	24	60

Steps	Example

Step 1. Prepare the axes, the x and y coordinates of the graph

Form two axes, one vertical and one horizontal, representing the two measures to be correlated. Label the x axis so as to include the range of values of one measure and the y axis to include the values of the other measure.

Visually, there should appear to be <u>about the same spread</u> for each measure between the highest and the lowest scores obtained, whether this is true numerically or not. If the difference between the highest and lowest scores on each measure is about the same, then the same scale value (e.g., one square = 5 points) should be used for both axes.

If, on the other hand, one of the measures has a score range that is, say, 1½ times greater than the obtained range of the other measure, then two different scales (e.g., one square = 6 points vertically; one square = 4 points horizontally) should be used so that both axes will be of similar length.

Step 1. Prepare the axes, the x and y coordinates of the graph

The obtained scores range from 12 to 49 on the SPM and from 40 to 83 on the reading test. Allowing leeway above and below, the horizontal axis for SPM ranges from 0 to 60. The vertical axis for the reading test ranges from 30 to 90 so that it includes the obtained scores.

It is all right to use the same scale (one square = 10 points) for both axes, since both measures had approximately the same spread between their highest and lowest scores—that is, a spread of 47 on the SPM and a spread of 43 on the reading test.

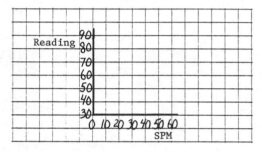

Step 2. Plot the data

Plot the data by putting dots at the intersections representing each pair of scores. There is one dot for each person or case. A single dot illustrates the scores on each of the two measures. If a pair of scores recurs, circle the dot.

Step 2. Plot the data

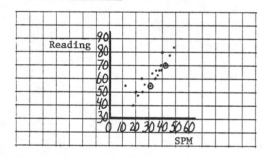

Step 3. Examine the graph

Examine the graph to see if there is a linear trend or if there appears to be a clear curve.

Step 3. Examine the graph

There is a strong linear trend, a narrow cigar-like shape, showing the two sets of scores to be related.

Step 4. Interpret the graph thus far

a. A set of points which forms a <u>circular</u> spread will not yield a high correlation, and in such a case you may wish to terminate your investigation of the relationship at this point.

Step 4. Interpret the graph thus far

The coordinator decided that the SPM was a good predictor of achievement.

Steps	Example

b. A set of points which forms a <u>cigar shape</u> is promising as far as yielding a significant correlation. The thinner the cigar, the more likely the correlation is to be a strong one.

Weak correlation: | Strong positive correlation: | Strong negative correlation:

c. A curved cigar, or banana shaped set of points, may or may not be worth investigating further depending upon the amount of curvature. For example:

 Calculation of r is <u>not</u> appropriate here since a straight line relationship is misleading.

  In this case, calculation of r <u>is</u> acceptable since there is a linear, straight line <u>trend</u> despite some curvature.

<u>Step 5. If the scores produce a cigar shape, graph the best straight line, also known as a regression line</u>

On the graph of scores, locate the best straight line for the cigar.

One way to place the line is to use a piece of thread. When you are adjusting the thread's position, imagine that each dot on the graph is attached to the thread by a rubber band. Put the thread into the position you think would best balance the thread between the scores. Then draw the line in that position.

<u>Step 5. If the scores produce a cigar shape, graph the best straight line, also known as a regression line</u>

The coordinator graphed the regression line, showing a positive correlation that looked potentially high, as shown here:

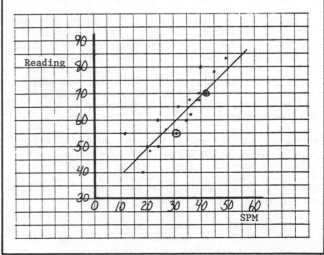

Worksheet 4B

Pearson's Product Moment Correlation Coefficient

Steps	Example

PREVIEW

The formula for computing this correlation coefficient is:

$$r = \frac{n(sumXY) - (sumX)(sumY)}{\sqrt{[n \cdot sum(X^2)-(sumX)^2][n \cdot sum(Y^2)-(sumY)^2]}}$$

where X represents scores on one measure, Y represents scores on the other, and n is the total number of pairs of scores. Do not be alarmed by the size of this formula. The following steps should make computation of this formula easy to follow.

Step 1. Prepare a table

To calculate this particular r, you start with two sets of scores from one set of cases. Call the two sets of scores the X and Y scores. Write down in a column the names of cases for whom you have scores. Usually, this column contains students' names. If your scores were classroom averages, though, you would identify classrooms in this column. The number of cases for whom you have both scores is n.

Cross out any person for whom you do not have both scores. Examine both sets of scores carefully to make sure that this loss of cases does not represent a systematic effect that will bias your results. In any event, loss of data will have to be reported with your results.

Background

An evaluator suspected that some students were not doing well on the word problems test in a mathematics achievement battery because they could not read. He decided to check the correlation between reading grade placement scores and the word problems score. He collected data from a random sample of students. Shown here are just 10 of the scores:

Student	Word problems test scores	Reading test raw scores
John	14	58
Jane	9	40
Julie	8	42
Jack	10	38
Linda	11	40
Len	5	42
Lucille	6	40
Larry	13	50
Nina	7	30
Terry	8	34

Step 1. Prepare a table

	Steps		Example

Now, make a table with 5 columns. Label the additional columns as shown below, and enter the X and Y scores in columns 2 and 4.

Cases	1 X^2	2 X	3 XY	4 Y	5 Y^2
1					
2					
3					
.					
.					
.					
Totals n=	A=	B=	C=	D=	E=
		$B^2=$		$D^2=$	

Step 2. Fill in the table

a. Fill in column 1. Square the X score from column 2, and put the result on the same row in column 1. To square a number, multiply the number by itself. At the bottom of the column, add up all the values to get the sum, A. It is sum(X^2) from the formula.

b. Complete column 2. At the bottom of the column, add up all the X scores to give the sum, B. It is sumX from the formula. Underneath, write down what B^2 comes to, (B·B). B^2 is (sumX)^2.

c. Fill in column 3. Multiply the X score from column 2 by the Y score from column 4, and enter this XY value in column 3. At the bottom of the column, add up all the values. Call their sum C. It is sumXY.

d. Complete column 4. At the bottom of the column, add up all the Y scores to give their sum, D. Underneath, write down what D^2 comes to. D^2 is (sumY)^2.

e. Fill in column 5. Square the Y score from column 4, and enter the result in column 5. At the bottom of the column, add up all the Y^2 values to get their sum, E. E is sum(Y^2).

Step 3. Compute r

You now have all the numbers you need to compute r. This is the formula:

$$ r = \frac{[n \cdot C] - [B \cdot D]}{\sqrt{[n \cdot A - B^2][n \cdot E - D^2]}} $$

The word problems scores are entered in column 2, and the reading test scores are entered in column 4.

Student	1 X^2	2 X	3 XY	4 Y	5 Y^2
John		14		58	
Jane		9		40	
Julie		8		42	
Jack		10		38	
Linda		11		40	
Len		5		42	
Lucille		6		40	
Larry		13		50	
Nina		7		30	
Terry		8		34	

Step 2. Fill in the table

a to e.

Student	1 X^2	2 X	3 XY	4 Y	5 Y^2
John	196	14	812	58	3364
Jane	81	9	360	40	1600
Julie	64	8	336	42	1764
Jack	100	10	380	38	1444
Linda	121	11	440	40	1600
Len	25	5	210	42	1764
Lucille	36	6	240	40	1600
Larry	169	13	650	50	2500
Nina	49	7	210	30	900
Terry	64	8	272	34	1156
Totals n=10	A=905	B=91	C=3910	D=414	E=17692
		$B^2=8281$		$D^2=171396$	

Step 3. Compute r

Steps	Example

Here are the substeps to compute r:

a. Work out the brackets. Note that $n \cdot A - B^2$ is computed by first multiplying A by n, and then subtracting from the answer the quantity B·B.

a.
$$r = \frac{[10 \cdot 3910] - [91 \cdot 414]}{\sqrt{[10 \cdot 905 - 8281][10 \cdot 17692 - 171396]}}$$

$$r = \frac{[39100] - [37674]}{\sqrt{[769][5524]}}$$

b. Work out the top line, the numerator. It may be negative.

b.
$$r = \frac{1426}{\sqrt{[769][5524]}}$$

c. Compute the bottom line, the denominator, by multiplying the brackets, and then taking the square root.

c.
$$r = \frac{1426}{\sqrt{4247956}}$$

$$r = \frac{1426}{2061.05}$$

d. Divide the numerator by the denominator: the result is r which has to be between -1 and +1. If your result is less than -1 or greater than +1, then there has been an error, so check all work carefully until you locate the mistake. If the numerator was negative, r will be negative.

d.
$$r = 0.69$$

Step 4. Interpret the statistic

See the discussion beginning on page 92.

Step 4. Interpret the statistic

This exercise shows a high positive correlation. For the sake of illustration, however, the calculations were performed with scores from only 10 students. If the same correlation were to hold for the entire set of data, however, the evaluator could conclude: "A strong positive relationship was found between reading test and word problem scores."

Steps	Example

Steps

PREVIEW

$$r_s = 1 - \frac{6 \; sum(d^2)}{n(n^2-1)} \quad \text{where}$$

d = the difference between the rank on one measure (x) and the rank on the other measure (y)

n = number of cases

The steps for preparing the data and calculating r_s from the formula are presented on the following pages.

Example

Background

In a program which had as one of its goals the improvement of students' attitudes to mathematics, teachers urged the evaluator to take into consideration children's math achievement when interpreting their attitudes: "Those who can do it, like it," the teachers stated.

To test the validity of this statement, the evaluator computed, for each classroom, the correlation between children's liking for math (measured by a questionnaire) and their math rank in the class (based on teachers' records of classroom tests). Math ranks and questionnaire results are shown below for one classroom.

Student	Questionnaire score	Math rank in class
KA	30	10
JC	30	8
TC	28	9
WD	32	11
MF	36	3
KJ	34	6
CJ	30	5
PH	29	14
WK	35	4
AL	28	12
CM	27	15
LM	23	18
JT	34	2
MT	33	16
MV	38	7
TW	22	17
CW	35	1
DW	36	13
EW	29	20
SY	31	19

Steps	Example

Step 1. Prepare a data table

Show the rank of each case on each measure.

1 Case	2 Rank on Measure X	3 Rank on Measure Y
1 2 3 4 . . n		

If results are available not as <u>ranks</u> but as scores, then you must first rank order the scores, dealing with ties as described in Worksheet 3D, page 61.

Step 1. Prepare a data table

In order to put the scores into the proper form for calculating r_s, the evaluator turned the questionnaire scores into ranks. To do this, he wrote out the questionnaire scores in descending order, and then wrote the ranks next to the scores. He indicated tied scores by dots.

Questionnaire score	Rank
38	1
36 ·	2.5
35 ·	4.5
34 ·	6.5
33	8
32	9
31	10
30 ··	12
29 ·	14.5
28 ·	16.5
27	18
23	19
22	20

He now could fill in this table:

1 Student	2 Rank on Questionnaire	3 Math rank in class
KA	12	10
JC	12	8
TC	16.5	9
WD	9	11
MF	2.5	3
KJ	6.5	6
CJ	12	5
PH	14.5	14
WK	4.5	4
AL	16.5	12
CM	18	15
LM	19	18
JT	6.5	2
MT	8	16
MV	1	7
TW	20	17
CW	4.5	1
DW	2.5	13
EW	14.5	20
SY	10	19

	Steps		Example

Steps

Step 2. For each case, compute d and d^2

The difference between ranks on the two measures is d. To compute each d, subtract the rank in column 3 from the rank in column 2. Add two columns to the data table, and enter d and then d^2 on each row. Multiply d by itself to get d^2.

1 Case	2 Rank on Measure X	3 Rank on Measure Y	4 Difference in ranks d	5 d^2
1				
2				
3				
4				
.				
.				
.				
n				

$$\text{sum } d^2 =$$

Step 3. Compute 6 sum(d^2)

Add up all the d^2 terms to produce the total for column 5; then multiply this quantity by 6. Enter the result here:

$$\boxed{} = 6 \text{ sum}(d^2)$$

Step 4. Compute $n(n^2-1)$

a. Count the number of cases and record here:

$$\boxed{} = n$$

b. Multiply n by itself and subtract 1 from the result:

$$\boxed{} = n^2-1$$

c. Multiply the results of Substeps a and b and enter the result here:

$$\boxed{} = n(n^2-1)$$

Example

Step 2. For each case, compute d and d^2

1 Case	2 Rank on Measure X	3 Rank on Measure Y	4 Difference in ranks d	5 d^2
KA	12	10	2	4
JC	12	8	4	16
TC	16.5	9	7.5	56.25
WD	9	11	-2	4
MF	2.5	3	-0.5	0.25
KJ	6.5	6	0.5	0.25
CJ	12	5	7	49
PH	14.5	14	0.5	0.25
WK	4.5	4	0.5	0.25
AL	16.5	12	4.5	20.25
CM	18	15	3.0	9
LM	19	18	1.0	1
JT	6.5	2	4.5	20.25
MT	8	16	-8	64
MV	1	7	-6	36
TW	20	17	3	9
CW	4.5	1	3.5	12.25
DW	2.5	13	-10.5	110.25
EW	14.5	20	-5.5	30.25
SY	10	19	-9	81

$$\text{sum } d^2 = 523.50$$

Step 3. Compute 6 sum(d^2)

$$\text{sum } d^2 = 523.50$$

$$6 \ (523.50) = \boxed{3{,}141}$$

Step 4. Compute $n(n^2-1)$

a.

$$n = 20$$

b.

$$n^2-1 = 400 - 1 = 399$$

c.

$$n(n^2-1) = 20 \ (399) = \boxed{7{,}980}$$

Steps	Example

Steps

Step 5. Compute r_s

a. Divide the result of Step 3 by the final result in Step 4.

$$\boxed{} = \frac{6\ \text{sum}(d^2)}{n(n^2-1)}$$

b. Subtract the result from 1.00

$$\boxed{} = 1 - \frac{6\ \text{sum}(d^2)}{n(n^2-1)}$$

The result is r_s.

$$\boxed{} = r_s$$

Step 6. Interpret the statistic

Values of r_s beyond ±.80 (read "plus or minus" .80) indicate a very strong relationship; values beyond ±.40 generally represent a weak relationship.

Use Worksheet 4G and Figure 14, pages 116 and 118, to determine confidence limits around r. Though the figure applies strictly to correlation coefficients based on the Pearson r, it can be roughly applied to Spearman's r as well. For a discussion about interpreting confidence limits around r, see page 92.

Example

Step 5. Compute r_s

a.

$$\frac{3,141}{7,980} = .39$$

b.

$$1.00 - .39 = .61$$

$$r_s = \boxed{.61}$$

Step 6. Interpret the statistic

This correlation showed a fairly strong relationship and tended to confirm the teachers' suggestions that achievement _was_ related to attitudes in this situation. This finding helped the evaluator to interpret results of attitude measures.

Steps	Example

PREVIEW

You have two dichotomous measures. To calculate Ø (pronounced f$\overline{ee}$), you will summarize the data in a <u>contingency table</u> and then apply a formula to the values in the contingency table. The formula yields Ø, the correlation coefficient for dichotomous data.

Background

A school district was evaluating its teacher aide and parent volunteer program. Teachers maintained that the presence of aides and volunteers was helping students to succeed in school and was helping them to avoid social maladjustment and academic problems.

The evaluator decided to try a quick check on this contention. He asked the principals at several schools to obtain from third and fourth grade teachers a list of all students who presented problems for any reasons: they were truant, academically depressed, withdrawn, disinterested, etc. Meanwhile, he checked school records to locate which children had been in classrooms with volunteer aides or parent volunteers during first and second grade.

His list from a sample of students randomly drawn from all classes appears on the following page.

Steps	Example

Step 1. Prepare data

Prepare a table showing each, say, student's status on each of the two measures.

Case	Measure 1 1=yes 0=no	Measure 2 1=yes 0=no
1		
2		
3		
.		
.		
n		

Step 1. Prepare data

Student	Was the student in classes with aide/ volunteer for 1st and 2nd grade? 1=yes 0=no	Did 3rd or 4th grade teacher nominate him/her as a problem? 1=yes 0=no
BA	1	0
CA	1	0
DA	0	0
WA	0	0
XB	1	1
MB	0	0
JB	0	1
TB	0	1
PC	0	0
RC	1	0
TC	1	0
VD	0	1
XE	0	0
ZE	0	1
BF	0	0
PG	1	1
RH	1	0
SI	1	0
TJ	1	0
UK	0	0
VL	0	0
AW	0	1
AX	1	0
AY	0	1
AZ	0	1

Step 2. Make a contingency table

Transform the list from Step 1 into a <u>contingency table</u> by tallying each student in one of the four cells of the table.

Put a tally in this cell for each student with a 1 (yes) on Measure 1 and a 0 (no) on Measure 2

Put a tally in this cell for students with 1-1 on the measures

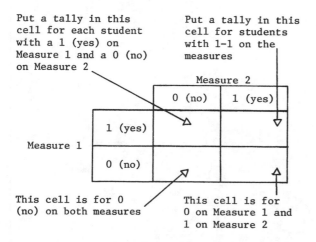

This cell is for 0 (no) on both measures

This cell is for 0 on Measure 1 and 1 on Measure 2

Step 2. Make a contingency table

		Problem?	
		0 (no)	1 (yes)
Teacher aide or parent volunteer?	1 (yes)	⫴⫲ ⦀	‖
	0 (no)	⫴⫲ ⦀	⫴⫲ ‖

Steps	Example

Step 3. Add marginals to the contingency table

Marginals are the sums of the rows and columns:

a	b	a+b = Y
c	d	c+d = Z

a+c = W   b+d = X

Step 4. Calculate Ø from this formula

$$\emptyset = \frac{b \cdot c - a \cdot d}{\sqrt{W \cdot X \cdot Y \cdot Z}}$$

Substeps for computing Ø:

a. Multiply b·c

b. Multiply a·d

c. Subtract the result of Substep b from the result of Substep a

d. Compute W·X·Y·Z

e. Find the square root of Substep d

f. Divide the result of Substep c by the result of Substep e to obtain Ø

[ ] = Ø

Step 3. Add marginals to the contingency table

a = 8	b = 2	Y = 10
c = 8	d = 7	Z = 15

W = 16   X = 9

Step 4. Calculate Ø from this formula

$$\emptyset = \frac{b \cdot c - a \cdot d}{\sqrt{W \cdot X \cdot Y \cdot Z}}$$

a.

    b·c = 16

b.

    a·d = 56

c.

    b·c − a·d = 16 − 56 = −40

d.

    W·X·Y·Z = 16·9·10·15 = 21,600

e.

    $\sqrt{W \cdot X \cdot Y \cdot Z} = \sqrt{21,600} = 146.97$

f.

    $\emptyset = \frac{-40}{146.97} = \boxed{-0.272}$

Steps	Example

Step 5. Interpret the statistic

The phi coefficient is interpreted like a normal correlation coefficient. Ignoring the sign, values less than 0.30 are weak; values above 0.60 are strong relationships.

Negative values indicate that <u>yes</u> on one measure is found more often with a <u>no</u> on the other measure. The measures are <u>negatively correlated</u>; there is an <u>inverse</u> relationship.

How firm the relationship is depends upon the number of cases, that is, the number of observations. Refer to Figure 14 in Worksheet 4G to check confidence limits.

Step 5. Interpret the statistic

The weak negative relationship (-0.27) from a small sample of students was not considered conclusive but was in the direction predicted by the teachers' contention: <u>yes</u> on one measure (<u>was</u> in classroom with teacher aide or parent volunteer) was associated with <u>no</u> on the second measure (<u>was not</u> a problem the following year).

The evaluator, therefore, aggregated all the data from third and fourth grade classrooms, obtaining the following contingency table and $\emptyset$ value:

		Problem?	
		0	1
Teacher aide or parent volunteer?	1	160	40
	0	140	160

$$\emptyset = \frac{5600 - 22{,}400}{\sqrt{3{,}024{,}000{,}000}}$$

$$= \frac{-16{,}800}{54{,}911}$$

$$\emptyset = \boxed{-.31}$$

This result was similar to what he obtained in the first place. Checking the confidence limits for this larger sample, however, showed this to be a firm result.

What did the evaluator know? He knew that students who occupied classrooms that had aides tended to have a better record of school adjustment. This did not mean that the presence of an aide <u>caused</u> better student adjustment--or vice versa. Some other factor might have brought about the relationship.

Perhaps particularly influential teachers got well-adjusted students as well as aides. Or maybe aides were concerned volunteer parents working in the classes of their own well-behaved children. In order to strengthen a case for a causal relationship between presence of aides and student adjustment, the evaluator must collect information to rule out such alternative explanations.

Rank Biserial
Correlation Coefficient

Steps	Example

Steps

PREVIEW

You have one ordinal measure and one dichotomous measure.

$$r_{rb} = \frac{2}{n} (\bar{R}_1 - \bar{R}_0) \quad \text{where}$$

n = total number ranked

$\bar{R}_1$ = mean rank of those in category 1 on the dichotomous measure

$\bar{R}_0$ = mean rank of those in category 0 on the dichotomous measure

This simple formula applies whenever there are <u>no tied ranks</u>. In the case of tied ranks, either toss a coin to break them and treat your result as a rough indication, or consult Cureton, E. E. Rank-biserial correlation when ties are present. <u>Educational and Psychological Measurement</u>, 1968, <u>28</u>, 77-79.

Example

Background

A committee consisting of board members, parents, teachers, and supervisors was considering the issue of whether or not to train elementary teachers in phonics methods. They demanded some "real evidence from <u>this</u> district" as to the effectiveness of phonics instruction.

One reading supervisor suggested that 20 children, randomly selected from a variety of phonics and non-phonics programs, read aloud to the committee. This was arranged, and the committee rank-ordered the children after hearing them each read several times.

The supervisor recorded the committee's ranks and then added information about which child had or had not been in a phonics program. The results which he put on the board at the committee meeting are shown on the following pages.

Steps	Example

Step 1. Prepare a case-rank-category table

For each case, record its rank on the ordinal measure and its category on the dichotomous measure.

1 Case	2 Ordinal rank	3 Dichotomous category
1		
2		
3		
4		
.		
.		
.		
n		

Step 1. Prepare a case-rank-category table

1 Child	2 Committee's rank of child	3 1 = in phonics 0 = not in phonics
Patrick	9	1
John	15	0
Jane	7	1
Susie	2	1
Cheryl	8	0
Pablo	6	1
LaVon	1	1
Tommy	16	0
Derek	18	0
Cornelius	14	1
Harrold	5	1
Brenda	3	1
Sharon	10	0
Brian	4	0
David	19	0
Carol	20	0
Lynne	17	0
Bryan	13	1
Aaron	11	1
Dick	12	0

Step 2. Compute $\overline{R}_1$ and $\overline{R}_0$, the mean rank of the cases in each of the two categories

a. List separately the ranks from column 2 of all cases which were placed in category 1 on the dichotomous variable--column 3 of the table. Compute the mean of these ranks.

$$\boxed{} = \overline{R}_1$$

b. Repeat for cases in category 0 of the dichotomous variables.

$$\boxed{} = \overline{R}_0$$

Step 2. Compute R_1 and R_0, the mean rank of the cases in each of the two categories

a & b.

Ranks of children in phonics program (1 in column 3 above)	Ranks of children not in phonics program (0 in column 3 above)
9	15
7	8
2	16
6	18
1	10
14	4
5	19
3	20
13	17
11	12
71	139

$$\overline{R}_1 = \frac{71}{10} = \boxed{7.1}$$ (Mean rank for children in phonics program)

$$\overline{R}_0 = \frac{139}{10} = \boxed{13.9}$$ (Mean rank for children not in phonics program)

Steps	Example

Step 3. Calculate r_{rb}

$$r_{rb} = \frac{2}{n}(\bar{R}_1 - \bar{R}_0)$$

$$r_{rb} = \frac{2}{n}\left[\begin{array}{c}\text{difference in}\\ \text{mean ranks}\end{array}\right]$$

Substeps for computing r_{rb}:

a. Subtract $\bar{R}_0$ from $\bar{R}_1$ (Step 2), and drop the sign if it is negative.

$$\boxed{} = \bar{R}_1 - \bar{R}_0$$

b. Divide 2 by the total number of cases

$$\boxed{} = \frac{2}{n}$$

c. Multiply the result of Substep a by the result of Substep b to obtain r_{rb}

$$\boxed{} = r_{rb}$$

Step 4. Interpret the statistic

You will notice that the rank biserial procedure outlined here always gives you a correlation coefficient that is positive. This is because showing the direction of relationship is not meaningful when one set of scores consists of dichotomous categories, sometimes chosen arbitrarily. You should interpret r_{rb} as lending an idea of the degree of relationship between rank and group membership.

Use Worksheet 4G, page 115, to calculate confidence limits and check the statistical significance of your result. If you should find that r_{rb} is statistically significant, then report that there seems to be a significant relationship between category membership and rank. Point out, as well, which group attained the highest ranks (the group with the lower $\bar{R}_x$).

Step 3. Calculate r_{rb}

a.

$$7.1 = 13.9 = \not{6}.8$$

b.

$$\frac{2}{20}$$

c.

$$\frac{2}{20}(6.8) = \boxed{0.68} = r_{rb}$$

Step 4. Interpret the statistic

Reference to Figure 14 in Worksheet 4G indicated that this was a statistically significant result. The reading supervisor emphasized that phonics children had been ranked higher than non-phonics children as shown by the difference in average ranks. The children had been randomly selected from each program and so were presumably fairly representative of the children in the programs. However, it could be that the children who were being taught phonics were the more able children, the supervisor conceded.

The committee was impressed by the demonstration in which they had participated. They asked the district evaluator to check math scores for children in the two kinds of reading programs to explore the possibility of differences in ability.

Steps	Example

PREVIEW

You have one dichotomous measure and one interval measure. The dichotomous measure can be thought of as having two responses, A or B. Suppose the respondents are divided into the A-group and the B-group on the basis of their response on the dichotomous measure. The interval scale yields a set of scores that can be called X scores.

The correlation coefficient is computed from this formula:

$$r_{pb} = \frac{(\overline{X}_A - \overline{X}_B)}{s} \cdot \sqrt{\frac{n_A \cdot n_B}{N(N-1)}} \quad \text{where}$$

$\overline{X}_A$ = the mean of the A-group on the interval measure

$\overline{X}_B$ = the mean of the B-group on the interval measure

s = the standard deviation of all the X scores

n_A = number in the A-group

n_B = number in the B-group

N = total number of cases ($N = n_A + n_B$)

Background

A questionnaire had been given to parents. From adding the responses to several items on the questionnaire, the general satisfaction of the parents with the school could be given a score.

The principal wondered if parents who had children in the Early Childhood Program (ECP) were more satisfied with the school than parents who did not have children in the ECP. Since one question at the end of the questionnaire was "Do you have a child in the ECP? (yes or no)," he was quickly able to divide the questionnaires into two piles: one for the yes responses (child in ECP), and the other for the no responses.

The table below shows a small sample of his data which will be used to illustrate his computations:

Parent number	Child in ECP?	Score on items measuring favorableness of attitude to school	
1	Yes	23	
2	Yes	15	
3	Yes	20	
4	Yes	19	
5	Yes	17	→ Sum=150
6	Yes	24	
7	Yes	16	
8	Yes	16	
9	No	15	
10	No	12	
11	No	10	
12	No	14	
13	No	13	→ Sum=112
14	No	20	
15	No	16	
16	No	12	

Steps	Example

Step 1. Compute the standard deviation of all scores on the interval measure

List all the X scores, that is, the scores on the interval measure. Use Worksheet 2E to compute the standard deviation of these scores. Record the result here, and record also the total number of scores.

$\boxed{}$ = s

$\boxed{}$ = N

Step 2. Compute $\overline{X}_A$ and $\overline{X}_B$

Separate the cases into two groups on the basis of the dichotomous variable. Let A be one group and B be the other.

For each group, record the number in the group and their mean score.

$\boxed{}$ = n_A

$\boxed{}$ = $\overline{X}_A$

$\boxed{}$ = n_B

$\boxed{}$ = $\overline{X}_B$

Step 3. Substitute the values recorded in Steps 1 and 2 into the formula to compute r_{pb}

Here are the substeps to compute r_{pb}:

a. Multiply n_A by n_B

$\boxed{}$ = $n_A \cdot n_B$

Step 1. Compute the standard deviation of all scores on the interval measure

The principal made a list of the attitude to school scores from both piles and used Worksheet 2E to compute the standard deviation. He recorded the result as well as the total number of scores:

s = $\boxed{3.84}$

N = $\boxed{16}$

Step 2. Compute $\overline{X}_A$ and $\overline{X}_B$

The X scores in each pile--the yes pile and the no pile for the ECP question--were summed. The sum of all the scores in the yes pile was 150. In the no pile the sum of the X's was 112. Each number was then divided by the number of questionnaires in the pile to obtain the mean for the set of scores.

Here are the principal's notes:

n_A = 8 = number of <u>yes</u> responses

$\dfrac{\text{Sum } X_A}{n_A}$ = $\dfrac{150}{8}$ = 18.75

$\overline{X}_A$ = $\boxed{18.75}$

n_B = 8 = number of <u>no</u> responses

$\dfrac{\text{Sum } X_B}{n_B}$ = $\dfrac{112}{8}$ = 14

$\overline{X}_B$ = $\boxed{14}$

Step 3. Substitute the values recorded in Steps 1 and 2 into the formula to compute r_{pb}

a.

$n_A \cdot n_B$ = 8·8 = 64

Steps	Example

b. Multiply N (see Step 1 for N) by the number which is one less than N

$$\boxed{} = N(N-1)$$

b.

$$N(N-1) = 16 \cdot 15 = 240$$

c. Divide the result of Substep a by the result of Substep b

$$\boxed{} = \frac{n_A \cdot n_B}{N(N-1)}$$

c.

$$\frac{n_A \cdot n_B}{N(N-1)} = \frac{64}{240} = .266$$

d. Take the square root of the result of Substep c

$$\boxed{} = \sqrt{\frac{n_A \cdot n_B}{N(N-1)}}$$

d.

$$\sqrt{\frac{n_A \cdot n_B}{N(N-1)}} = \sqrt{.266} = .516$$

e. Subtract $\overline{X}_B$ from $\overline{X}_A$

$$\boxed{} = \overline{X}_A - \overline{X}_B$$

e.

$$\overline{X}_A - \overline{X}_B = 18.75 - 14.00 = 4.75$$

f. Divide the result of Substep e by s which was found in Step 1. If Substep e gave a negative result, this Substep will be negative as well.

$$\boxed{} = \frac{\overline{X}_A - \overline{X}_B}{s}$$

f.

$$\frac{\overline{X}_A - \overline{X}_B}{s} = \frac{4.75}{3.84} = 1.237$$

g. Multiply the result of Substep f by the result of Substep d. The answer will be negative if Substep e gave a negative result. The result is r_{pb}.

$$\boxed{} = r_{pb} \quad \text{(the point biserial correlation coefficient)}$$

g.

$$1.237 \cdot 0.516 = .638$$

$$r_{pb} = \boxed{.64}$$

Step 4. Interpret the statistic

See the text beginning on page 92.

Step 4. Interpret the statistic

A correlation of 64 was found to be a fairly hefty one, and one not likely to have occurred by chance. There indeed did seem to be a relationship between parental satisfaction and having a child in the Early Childhood Program.

Steps	Example

BACKGROUND AND PREVIEW

It is assumed that you have already computed some
correlation coefficient, r, between two measures,
and that these measures are based on n cases
(individuals, classes, schools, items).

Based upon these numbers, r and n, you first
approximate the <u>lower limit</u>, and then the <u>upper
limit</u>, of a 95% confidence interval around r by
using the charts on pages 116 and 118.

First, figure out the lower confidence limit:

<u>Step 1. Using Figure 14a on the next page, find
the best vertical line to represent your obtained
value of r</u>

Write down the obtained value of r, rounded off to
the nearest hundredth:

 = r

Look at the <u>horizontal</u> axis. Find the point on
the axis that most closely corresponds to your
obtained r. Is the point quite close to one of
the vertical lines? If so, then use the vertical
line to represent your r.

If not, then take a ruler and draw in your best
approximation of a vertical line rising up from
the point on the horizontal axis that corresponds
to your r. The line you have drawn represents
your r.

BACKGROUND

A correlation of .61 was found between a math
achievement test and the average number of minutes
per week spent on math instruction in 13 classrooms. The evaluator wanted to estimate a confidence interval around +.61 in order to find out
how much the obtained r might vary if the same
study were performed again. In this way, she
would determine whether much confidence could be
placed in +.61 as an estimate of the correlation,
or whether this result based on 13 cases was too
shaky to merit much attention.

<u>Step 1. Using Figure 14a on the next page, find
the best vertical line to represent your obtained
value of r</u>

r = | +.61 |

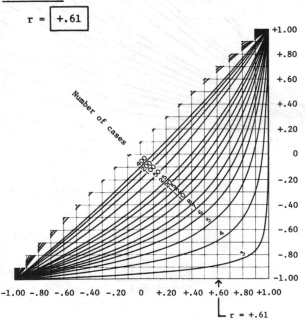

Since +.61 is so close to +.60, the line rising
up from .60 in the chart was used to represent
the obtained r.

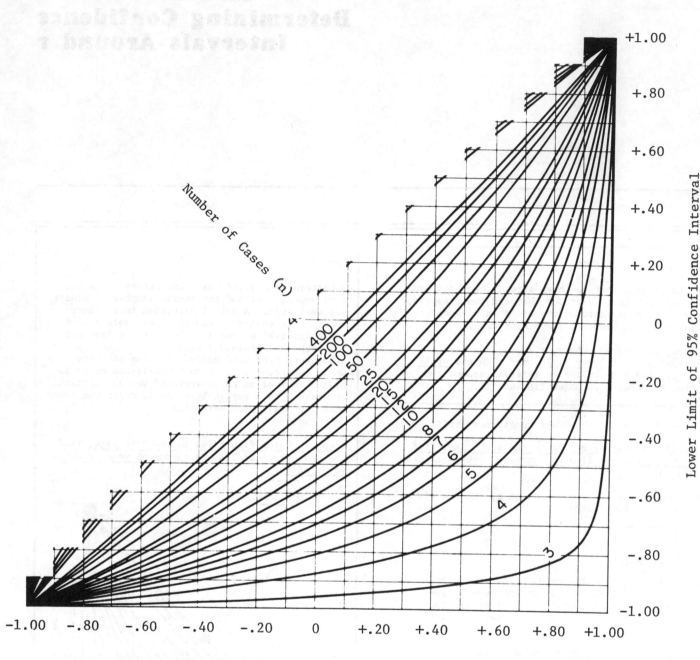

Number of Cases (n)

Lower Limit of 95% Confidence Interval

Obtained Correlation Coefficient

Figure 14a. Lower confidence limit, 95% confidence interval, determined by value of r and group size

Steps	Example

Step 2. Find the curve that is labeled with your number of cases, n

Write down the number of cases, n, used to compute r.

[   ] = n

Each curve in Figure 14a is labeled with a number. If one of the curves is labeled with your n, then that curve is the one you are looking for.

If your n is greater than 400, then use the curve labeled 400.

If your n is between two of the n's represented by curves, then use <u>both</u> of those curves in Step 3. That will give you <u>two</u> answers for the lower confidence limit, and you then must interpolate—that is, find a value between those two answers, a value that reflects how much closer your n is to either of the nearest labeled n's.

Step 2. Find the curve that is labeled with your number of cases, n

n = [13]

Since no curve is labeled 13, the evaluator took note of the curve marked 12 and the curve marked 15, since 13 is between 12 and 15.

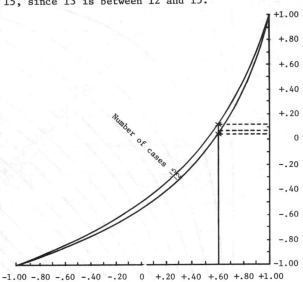

Step 3. Locate the lower confidence limit

Mark an X at the point of intersection of the vertical line (Step 1) and the curve (Step 2). Ask yourself: How high is this point in terms of the scale on the <u>vertical</u> axis?

If the point is <u>on</u> one of the horizontal lines, then read off the corresponding value for that line from the vertical axis. That value is your lower confidence limit.

If the point lies <u>between</u> two successive horizontal lines, then use a ruler to find the point on the vertical axis that is at the same height as the point of intersection. Estimate to the nearest hundredth the height of that point on the vertical axis. That estimation is your lower confidence limit.

[   ] = lower confidence limit

Following Steps 4 through 6, you will now calculate the upper confidence limit.

Step 3. Locate the lower confidence limit

A mark was made at the point where the line for r, rising from +.60, meets the 12-curve. Another mark was made at the point where the r-line meets the 15-curve. Using a ruler, the evaluator found the points on the vertical axis at the same height as the two marked points. Their values were estimated to be +.03 for the 12-curve and +.12 for the 15-curve.

Since <u>13 is one-third of the way between 12 and 15</u>, the evaluator chose +.06 as her estimate for the lower confidence limit, since .06 is one-third of the way from .03 to .12.

lower confidence limit = [+.06]

Obtained Correlation Coefficient

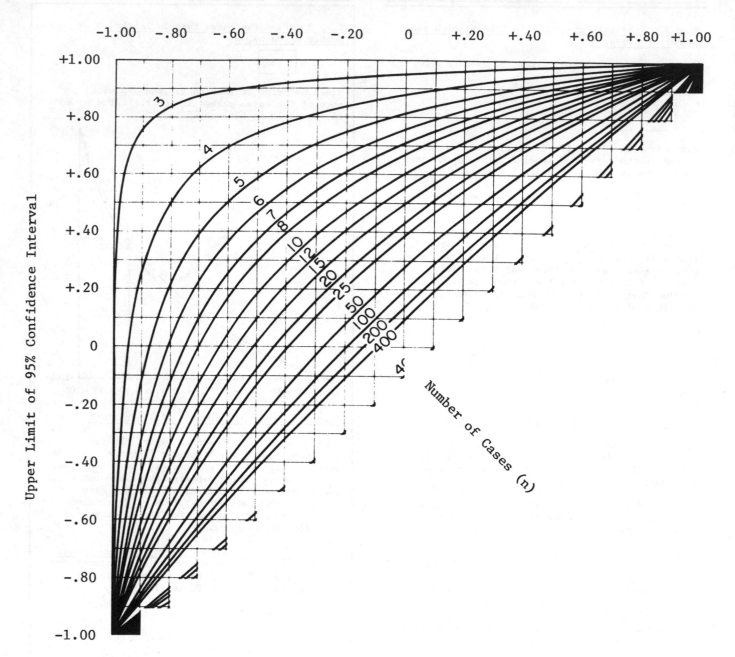

Figure 14b. Upper confidence limit, 95% confidence interval, determined by value of r and group size

Steps	Example

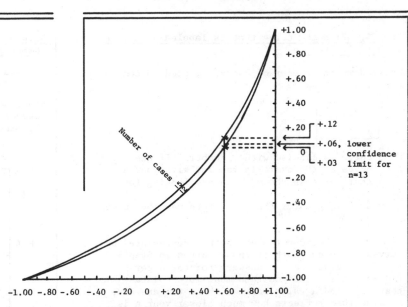

Step 4. Using Figure 14b on the facing page, find the best vertical line to represent your obtained value of r

Write down the obtained value of r, rounded off to the nearest hundredth.

   = r

Look at the horizontal axis at the top of the figure. Find the point on the axis that most closely corresponds to your obtained r. Is the point quite close to one of the vertical lines? If so, then use that vertical line to represent your r.

If not, then take a ruler and draw in your best approximation of a vertical line descending from the point on the horizontal axis that corresponds to your r. The line you have drawn represents your r.

Step 4. Using Figure 14b on the facing page, find the best vertical line to represent your obtained value of r

r = | +.61 | r = +.61 ⌐

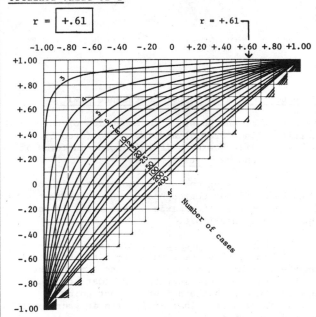

Since +.61 is so close to +.60, the line descending from .60 on the chart was used to represent the obtained r.

Steps	Example

Step 5. Find the curve that is labeled with your number of cases, n

Write down the number of cases, n, used to compute r.

$$\boxed{} = n$$

Each curve is labeled with a number. If one of the curves in the chart is labeled with your n, then that curve is the one you are looking for.

If your n is greater than 400, then use the curve labeled 400.

If your n is between two of the n's represented by curves, then use <u>both</u> of those curves in Step 6. That will give you <u>two</u> answers for the upper confidence limit, and you then must interpolate—that is, find a value between those two answers, a value that reflects how much closer your n is to either of the nearest labeled n's.

Step 6. Locate the upper confidence limit

Mark an X at the point of intersection of the vertical line (Step 4) and the curve (Step 5). Ask yourself: How high is this point in terms of the scale on the <u>vertical</u> axis?

If the point is <u>on</u> one of the horizontal lines, then read off the corresponding value for that line from the vertical axis. That value is your upper confidence limit.

If the point lies <u>between</u> two successive horizontal lines, then use a ruler to find the point on the vertical axis that is at the same height as the point of intersection. Estimate to the nearest hundredth the height of that point on the vertical axis. That estimation is your upper confidence limit.

$$\boxed{} = \text{upper confidence limit}$$

Step 5. Find the curve that is labeled with your number of cases, n

n = $\boxed{13}$

Since no curve is labeled 13, the evaluator took note of the curve marked 12 and the curve marked 15, since 13 is between 12 and 15.

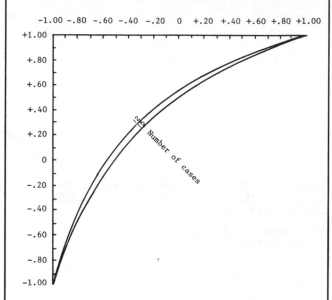

Step 6. Locate the upper confidence limit

Marks were made where the +.60 line for r meets the 12-curve and the 15-curve. Using a ruler, the evaluator found the points on the vertical axis at the same height as the two marked points. Their values were estimated at +.84 for the 15-curve and +.86 for the 12-curve.

Remember that 13 is one third of the way between 12 and 15, so the evaluator had to interpolate. One third of the distance between .84 and .86 is .007. Therefore, the upper confidence limit is .007 away from the 12-curve value, +.86, toward +.84. This is +.853. Rounding off to the nearest hundredth yields +.85, the upper confidence limit.

upper confidence limit = $\boxed{+.85}$

Steps   Example

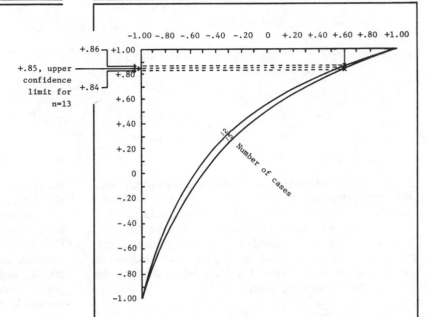

| +.85, upper confidence limit for n=13 |

Step 7. Describe and interpret the confidence interval

Write a summary statement explaining that the 95% confidence interval for r extends from the lower to the upper limit that you estimated from the charts. Thus, there is a 95% likelihood that this interval includes the true r--the average r you would get if the study were replicated again and again.

The wider the confidence interval, of course, the more doubtful your obtained r becomes. Thus, when 8 cases produce a correlation of +.45, your interval stretches from -.35 to +.85. The confidence interval begins at a weak negative value, goes through zero, and ends up at a high positive value. With such results, you cannot confidently say much at all about the true correlation between the two measures in the study!

On the other hand, if 8 cases produce a correlation of +.95, your interval only goes from +.75 to +.98, so you can have confidence that the true correlation is a fairly high positive one. Similarly, if 200 cases produce a correlation of +.45, your interval only goes from +.33 to +.55, so you can be confident that the true correlation is positive, and weak to moderate in magnitude.

Step 7. Describe and interpret the confidence interval

The confidence interval extends from +.06 to +.85. Because the confidence interval only includes positive values and excludes zero, the evaluator concluded that a correlation significantly greater than zero exists between scores on this math achievement test and time spent on math instruction with classes of students like those in this study.

The evaluator then referred to an educational theory that emphasized the importance of "time on task" in the learning of new skills. According to the theory, the true correlation should be moderately to highly positive. Although the r obtained in this study, +.61, was consistent with the theory, the evaluator admitted that the broad range of values included in the confidence interval--from barely above zero to a high positive value--provided no strong evidence for or against the theory.

The Chi-square test is only used with measures which place cases into categories. The test indicates whether the results from the two measures are about what one would expect if the two were *not* related. An example will make this clear. Suppose one measure classifies cases into *program categories*—students are in either the E-group math program or the C-group math program. There are 80 students in the E-group and 100 in the C-group:

Math Program Category

E-group   C-group

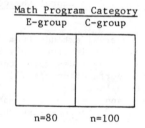

n=80   n=100

Now suppose that among these students (80 + 100 = 180 total), you know that 45 have scored above the 75th percentile in math, 45 scored in the middle range, and 90 scored below the 25th percentile. Call these categories *high, medium,* and *low.* List these categories down the left-hand side of the table you are now building, and write down the total number in each group outside the table at the right-hand side:

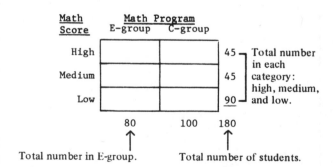

The numbers outside the box are called *marginals.* The blank boxes form a *contingency table,* displaying the num-

ber of students in each category. Now, what do you expect the numbers filling the cells will turn out to be? If there were *no* relationship between a student's math program and his score category, then, for the 80 students in the E-group, you would expect about 20 to be scoring high, 20 scoring medium, and 40 scoring low. Why? Because these figures—20, 20, and 40—would keep the figures inside the contingency table consistent with the proportions in the marginals—45, 45, 90. Thus the *expected distribution,* if math program and math scores were not related, would look like Table 3.

TABLE 3
Expected Distributions, Math Program

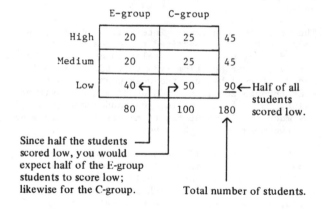

Note how the same frequency *pattern* runs down both columns in the contingency table and down the marginal column at the right. Even though the E- and C-groups have a different number of members, the *proportions* of these members form the same distribution pattern as the marginal. Since the two programs have produced the *same* scoring pattern, neither can be said to affect the trend of the results. There is no significant difference between them.

But what if the E-group were doing better than the C-group in math; that is, what if the experimental program *were* making a difference? Then leaving the marginals *the same,* perhaps the scores would look like Table 4.

TABLE 4
Observed Distributions, Math Program

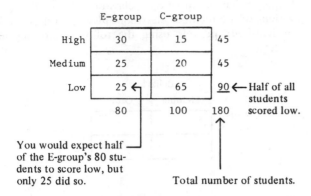

	E-group	C-group	
High	30	15	45
Medium	25	20	45
Low	25 ←	65	90 ← Half of all students scored low.
	80	100	180

You would expect half of the E-group's 80 students to score low, but only 25 did so.

Total number of students.

Overall, half the students are in the low math category, but in the E-group the proportion is much less than half, only 25 out of 80.

A Chi-square test compares the observed distributions with the distributions which would be expected if there were no relationship between the two sets of categories. Here, the test would compare Table 4 with Table 3. The test shows whether the *observed distribution* is sufficiently different from the *expected distribution* to be an unlikely occurrence. Something happening to E-group members—possibly, but not necessarily Program E—caused a difference in results.

When to Use Chi-Square

Make up a contingency table and apply the Chi-square test whenever you want to decide whether membership in one category has any bearing on membership in another: Is gender related to having blue, brown, or "other colored" eyes? Do teachers' judgments of whether a program is going poorly, well, or just average relate to whether their class size is small, medium, or large? The numbers contained in each cell of the Chi-square table always represent a tally of how many cases have the features named in the column and row headings for that cell. Here are some examples of questions that might be asked and the contingency tables which you would set up to answer them.

Examples

QUESTIONS	CONTINGENCY TABLES		
Were E-group and C-group teachers about equivalent in years of teaching experience?	Years Teaching	Program E-group	C-group
	less than 2		
	2 to 6		
	over 6		

QUESTIONS	CONTINGENCY TABLES		
Did parents of E-group students attend about the same number of PTA meetings as parents of C-group students?	Meetings Attended	Program E-group	C-group
	0		
	1 or 2		
	3 or more		
Was the distribution of students attaining the objectives about the same in the E-group and C-group?	Objectives Mastered	Program E-group	C-group
	90% or more		
	80 to 89%		
	70 to 79%		
	60 to 69%		
	50 to 59%		
	less than 50%		
Were the E-group and C-group similar in ethnic composition?	Ethnicity	Program E-group	C-group
	Black		
	Caucasian		
	Chicano		
	Oriental		
	Other		

Use of Chi-square is not limited by the number of categories defining either the columns or the rows, as the next examples show.

Examples

QUESTION: Were parents' attitudes toward the school's academic program related to the kind of reading program their children received?

CONTINGENCY TABLE:

Attitudes	Reading Program		
	Phonics	Experiential	Traditional
Favorable			
Unfavorable			
No response			

QUESTION: Are children in different classrooms expressing different career preferences?

CONTINGENCY TABLE:

Career Preferences	Classrooms 1	2	3	4
Professional				
White Collar				
Blue Collar				

Errors To Avoid When Using Chi-Square

The Chi-square test has often been inappropriately used. Asking the following questions will help you avoid errors:

1. *Are you sure that the categories naming the cells of your contingency table are well defined?* Have you eliminated ambiguities about which cell each case belongs in? Are the lines of demarcation between categories clear and definable?

2. *Does your contingency table include every possible category into which cases may fall?* Be particularly careful to include, where necessary, the category called "other" or that records absence of a characteristic. In the example mentioned earlier relating eye color and gender, merely looking at blue and brown-eyed people would produce an incomplete contingency table for detecting the relationship. The category "other colored" had to be included.

3. *Have you been careful to assure that, when making tallies in the cells of the table, each case (person, classroom, whatever) gets counted once and only once?* Counting the same case more than once is a common error when using Chi-square and is usually referred to as the error of repeated measures. Consider this example.

You want to know whether boys or girls exhibit more helping behaviors in an open classroom. You tally observations of a 6-member classroom playgroup during a set of half-hour periods using the following contingency table:

	Behaviors Helping	Other
Girls (n = 3)		
Boys (n = 3)		

You watch each child in turn for a 1-minute period, then tally whether the child seems to be helping or not. Your observations circle the group six times, giving you six observations per child. A Chi-square analysis is inappropriate in this situation, since the analysis is based on the assumption that each observation came from a different case; but your 36 observations did *not* come from 36 children. You can readily see that data based on 36 children would provide a sounder basis for drawing conclusions here than will data from 6 children!

A good way to ensure that you have not made a repeated-measures error is to look at the sum of the marginals of your contingency table. This sum should equal the number of cases in your study.

4. *Is the expected count in any one cell of the contingency table less than 5?* In the case of very small samples, other statistics with similar logical bases but different computations will need to be used. Consult a statistics text or ask a data analyst to help you.

Worksheet 4H
Chi-Square Test

Steps	Example

Steps

PREVIEW

You will make up two contingency tables for the same set of data: one table in which you record the observed distributions, and a second table in which you use the marginals to put down expected distributions. Then the numbers in these two tables are used to calculate a statistic called Chi-square. The bigger this number is, the more likely it is that there is a significant relationship between the two sets of categories.

Step 1. Draw up the observed contingency table from the raw data

Step 2. Make up the expected distributions using the marginals from the raw data

a. Set out the contingency table with only the observed marginals entered on the table. The marginals, you will remember, are the total numbers in each category. On the contingency table, these totals are written in the margins opposite the category to which they refer. The example shows a two by four contingency table, but you can use the same procedure for any size of table.

Example

Background

The evaluator of a preschool program wanted to test the hypothesis that children in Program E showed better adjustment to kindergarten than children who had no preschool experience.

Without telling teachers the purpose, he collected ratings from kindergarten teachers of each child's school adjustment. He then divided children into those who had and those who had not been in the preschool program and made up the contingency table shown in Step 1 below.

Step 1. Draw up the observed contingency table from the raw data

Adjustment:	Program E Preschool	Program C No preschool	
Excellent	40	60	100
Good	10	10	20
Fair	5	15	20
Poor	10	30	40
Very poor	15	45	60
	80	160	240

Step 2. Make up the expected distributions using the marginals from the raw data

a.

Steps	Example

Contingency Table

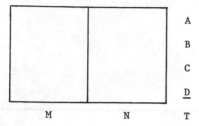

A

B

C

D

   M   N   T

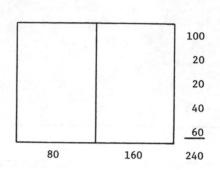

   80   160   240

T = total, which is equal to the sum of either set of marginals. Therefore,

$$T = A + B + C + D \quad \text{and}$$

$$T = M + N$$

b. Calculate the expected frequencies in the <u>first</u> column by computing the following:

$$\Big[\text{column total}\Big] \times \left[\frac{\text{row total}}{T}\right]$$

This yields the proportion of the column total expected from each row marginal. In the symbols shown for the above contingency table, the first entry in the first column is as shown:

$M \times \dfrac{A}{T}$		A
		B
		C
		<u>D</u>

    M   N   T

Filling in the whole first column, you have:

$M \times \dfrac{A}{T}$		A
$M \times \dfrac{B}{T}$		B
$M \times \dfrac{C}{T}$		C
$M \times \dfrac{D}{T}$		<u>D</u>

    M   N   T

b.

$80 \times \dfrac{100}{240}$		100
$80 \times \dfrac{20}{240}$		20
$80 \times \dfrac{20}{240}$		20
$80 \times \dfrac{40}{240}$		40
$80 \times \dfrac{60}{240}$		<u>60</u>

    80   160   240

Steps	Example

c. Fill in all the other columns using the same procedure for each cell:

$$\left[\text{column total} \right] \times \left[\frac{\text{row total}}{T} \right]$$

Thus:

$M \times \dfrac{A}{T}$	$N \times \dfrac{A}{T}$	A
$M \times \dfrac{B}{T}$	$N \times \dfrac{B}{T}$	B
$M \times \dfrac{C}{T}$	$N \times \dfrac{C}{T}$	C
$M \times \dfrac{D}{T}$	$N \times \dfrac{D}{T}$	D
M	N	T

c.

$80 \times \dfrac{100}{240}$	$160 \times \dfrac{100}{240}$	100
$80 \times \dfrac{20}{240}$	$160 \times \dfrac{20}{240}$	20
$80 \times \dfrac{20}{240}$	$160 \times \dfrac{20}{240}$	20
$80 \times \dfrac{40}{240}$	$160 \times \dfrac{40}{240}$	40
$80 \times \dfrac{60}{240}$	$160 \times \dfrac{60}{240}$	60
80	160	240

d. Complete the calculations in each cell, and assign each cell a number as in the example to the right. You now have a table of <u>expected frequencies</u>.

d.

1 33.33	6 66.67	100
2 6.67	7 13.33	20
3 6.67	8 13.33	20
4 13.33	9 26.67	40
5 20.00	10 40.00	60
80	160	240

<u>Step 3.</u> For each cell of the contingency table, compute this quantity:

$$\left[\frac{\overset{\text{observed}}{\text{frequency}} - \overset{\text{expected}}{\text{frequency}}}{\overset{\text{expected}}{\text{frequency}}} \right]^2$$

This can be written:

$$\frac{(O - E)^2}{E}$$

Note that the top quantity is squared.

It is convenient to work with a 6-columned table like the one shown in the example. Fill in the first three columns from the tables; then use the calculator. Work across each row. You really don't need to write down columns 4 and 5, but they are shown so you can check that you are working correctly.

Add up the <u>quantities</u> in column 6. The total is Chi-square, the required statistic. It has the symbol χ^2.

<u>Step 3.</u> For each cell of the contingency table, compute this quantity:

$$\left[\frac{\overset{\text{observed}}{\text{frequency}} - \overset{\text{expected}}{\text{frequency}}}{\overset{\text{expected}}{\text{frequency}}} \right]^2$$

1	2	3	4	5	6
Cell	O	E	O−E	$(O{-}E)^2$	$\dfrac{(O{-}E)^2}{E}$
1	40	33.33	6.67	44.5	1.33
2	10	6.67	3.33	11.1	1.66
3	5	6.67	−1.67	2.8	0.42
4	10	13.33	−3.33	11.1	0.83
5	15	20.00	−5.00	25.0	1.25
6	60	66.67	−6.67	44.5	0.67
7	10	13.33	−3.33	11.1	0.83
8	15	13.33	1.67	2.8	0.21
9	30	26.67	3.33	11.1	0.42
10	45	40.00	5.00	25.0	0.63

$$\chi^2 = 8.25$$

Steps	Example

Step 4. Check whether your Chi-square value is larger than the tabled Chi-square

To do this, first you need to figure out a number which you need in order to use the Chi-square table: the df number--degrees of freedom. To find the df number, imagine a row and a column from the contingency table are blotted out and count the number of remaining cells. The number is the df number.

Samples:

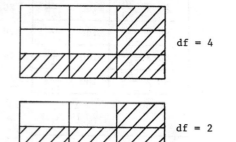

Now locate the tabled Chi-square by going down the left column to the appropriate df number, then selecting the Chi-square value from one of the columns.

df	Test at 10% error level	More stringent test (5% level)
1	2.71	3.84
2	4.60	5.99
3	6.25	7.81
4	7.79	9.49
5	9.24	11.07
6	10.64	12.59
7	12.02	14.07
8	13.36	15.51
9	14.68	16.92
10	15.99	18.31
11	17.27	19.67
12	18.55	21.03
13	19.81	22.36
14	21.06	23.68
15	22.31	25.00
16	23.54	26.30
17	24.77	27.59
18	25.99	28.87
19	27.20	30.14
20	28.41	31.41
21	29.61	32.67
22	30.81	33.92
23	32.01	35.17
24	33.20	36.41
25	34.38	37.65

Step 4. Check whether your Chi-square value is larger than the tabled Chi-square

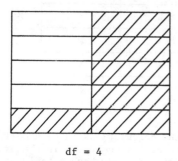

df = 4

For 4 degrees of freedom (in Column 1), the tabled Chi-square for a 10% error level is 7.79.

	Column 1	Column 2
df	Test at 10% error level	More stringent test (5% level)
1	2.71	3.84
2	4.60	5.99
3	6.25	7.81
4	(7.79)	9.49
5	9.24	11.07
6	10.64	12.59
7	12.02	14.07
8	13.36	15.51
9	14.68	16.92
10	15.99	18.31
11	17.27	19.67
12	18.55	21.03
13	19.81	22.36
14	21.06	23.68
15	22.31	25.00
16	23.54	26.30
17	24.77	27.59
18	25.99	28.87
19	27.20	30.14
20	28.41	31.41
21	29.61	32.67
22	30.81	33.92
23	32.01	35.17
24	33.20	36.41
25	34.38	37.65

Steps	Example

Example

Tabled χ^2 = 7.79 (at 10% error level)

Obtained χ^2 = 8.25 (from Step 3)

The obtained Chi-square is <u>larger</u> and therefore significant at this level. Notice that the tabled Chi-square for the 5% error level is 9.49. The obtained value is <u>less than</u> 9.49 and would therefore <u>not</u> be significant if the more demanding 5% criterion were applied.

Steps

Step 5. Interpret and report the statistic

If your obtained value of Chi-square is greater than that in the table, you can conclude that there is a relationship between the category that defines the columns and that which defines the rows. This can be reported by displaying the contingency table, recording Chi-square (χ^2) underneath it, and commenting in the text: "Analysis of Table ( ) showed there was a statistically significant relationship between ( ) and ( )."

<u>However</u>, do remember that correlation is not causation. A significant Chi-square test only establishes a statistical relationship. It does not tell you which categories are influencing which, if any. The relationship might occur because both sets of distributions are related to something else.

Sometimes you will find a significant χ^2 value and wonder if there was a strong relationship among all categories in the rows and columns or if <u>some particular subset of categories</u> caused the significant relationship. To examine this question, check Column 6 of the table in Step 3. If all cells had roughly equal values, then the significant Chi-square probably did not result from the influence of any particular cells. On the other hand, if most cells had small values but there were just one or two comparatively large values, then it is among these large values that you might find the source of the significant relationship.

Step 5. Interpret and report the statistic

The evaluator reported the observed frequencies, adding the percentage of students who had attended or not attended preschool, in the following way:

Table A
Reported Adjustment To School of Children
Who Did or Did Not Attend the Preschool Program

Adjustment:	Preschool		No preschool	
	number	%	number	%
Excellent	40	50.00	60	37.50
Good	10	12.50	10	6.25
Fair	5	6.25	15	9.40
Poor	10	12.50	30	18.70
Very poor	15	18.75	45	28.10
	80	100.00	160	100.00

Obtained Chi-square = 8.25

Tabled Chi-square = 7.79

He noted:

"Of the 80 children who attended preschool, 50% received a rating of <u>excellent</u> in adjustment to school as compared to only about 37% of those who did not attend preschool.

"This fact and others in Table A indicate that former preschoolers are showing better adjustment to school. A Chi-square test showed the adjustment differences between preschoolers and non-preschoolers to be significantly greater than could be due to chance alone, using a 10% chance of error.

"One interpretation of these findings is that preschool experiences helps a child to adjust to school later, at least in the eyes of the teacher. However, since preschool was voluntary and required some participation from mothers, it may be that children enrolled in preschool came from more concerned homes, and this was the factor causing their subsequent better attitudes to school, not the preschool experience itself."

Steps	Example

Another example of an evaluation employing a Chi-square test

An experimental program aimed at reducing school dropout rate was being evaluated.

Last September, the program coordinator had identified 150 9th-, 10th-, and 11th-graders as potential dropouts by looking at grades, behavior in school, and several socio-economic status and family background indicators. These students were randomly assigned to control and experimental groups. The experimental program consisted of special counseling, tutoring, and liaison work with parents throughout the school year.

The following September, the evaluator checked whether the students were still in school and reported the following:

Students:	Experimental number	%	Control number	%
In school	73	91.25	52	74.29
Could not be traced	1	1.25	3	4.29
Dropped out	6	7.50	15	21.43
	80	100.00	70	100.00

Obtained Chi-square = 7.74

Tabled Chi-square = 4.60

The table indicates that differences in stay/dropout between the two groups was significant, using a 10% chance of error. In fact, the dropout rate of the experimental group was about one-third that of the control group.

Chapter 5
Using Computers To Analyze Data: The SPSS System

In order to use a computer, you no longer need to know how computers work, or even how to program. You can now use ready-made computer programs, called *canned programs,* or *software packages,* to conduct the sorts of statistical tests described in this book—and many more. Some more advanced statistics, which require a computer, will be described below. How to use these programs can be learned quite simply by finding and reading a booklet called a *documentation.* The documentation is a manual which describes the programs available within a certain package and how to use them. Each computer center generally has a users' workroom in which various documentation manuals are kept for reference.

One of the most widely used collections of canned programs is the *Statistical Package for the Social Sciences* (SPSS).[17] The SPSS system has an excellent manual from which you can learn most of what you need to know in order to run data analyses by computer. This chapter is intended to serve as an introduction to the SPSS system.

What You Should Know About Data Analysis by Computer

If the study you are doing has more than 60 cases or if you are using more than three or four measurements with a smaller number of cases, it will become desirable to process the data by computer rather than by hand, even if the hand is assisted by a calculator. In fact, no matter what the size of your data set, becoming familiar with computer analysis is valuable. Nothing else so rapidly increases your competence to explore and analyze data.

There are two ways your data analysis can proceed:

1. You can find a knowledgeable assistant to feed data to and gather it from the computer. In this case, your main reason for reading this section will be to learn *what to ask for* and *how to provide the data* in a form appropriate for computer analysis.

2. You (yes, you) yourself can handle the entire data analysis operation, including the submission of *jobs* (data analysis requests) to the computer.

---

17. Nie, N. H., Hull, C. H., Jenkins, J. G., Steinbrenner, K., & Bent, D. H. *Statistical package for the social sciences (2nd ed.).* New York: McGraw-Hill, 1975.

If you are planning to do data analyses yourself, the following information should help prepare you for the indifferent, bustling, and sometimes confusing world of the computer center. Fortunately, most computer centers have a staff of consultants who are regularly on duty to answer questions about idiosyncracies in the procedures of a particular place. If you are in doubt about proper procedures, start asking questions from fellow users or from the staff.

If you are planning to have an assistant perform the computer analysis, most of the information below will be peripheral to your needs; but pay particular attention to the section *Preparing Data for Computer Analysis.*

Obtaining an Account, an Output Bin, and a Password

Learning how to use the computer is fruitless if you do not have an account. You will usually present data to the computer punched onto the familiar *do not fold, bend, or staple* cards, one of which is shown in Figure 17, page 133. Before the computer will look at any of *your* data cards, however, it must see a card meant for its own records that presents a valid charge number identifying the account you have established. Because private individuals are rarely able to buy computer time, you will probably have to purchase time in the name of the organization for which you work.

At the time you receive an *account number,* you may also be assigned an *output bin*—a place at the computer center to which your results will be sent when the computer has produced them. A *password* will also be assigned. You are advised to change it periodically to a word that only you know, to protect your account from use by others. There will be a desk or office at the computer center to assist you in establishing an account, and finding your output bin and password.

Keypunching

Before you give your data to the computer for analysis, it has to be punched onto cards. A *keypunch machine* (Figure 15) is a typewriter that punches holes in cards instead of printing words.

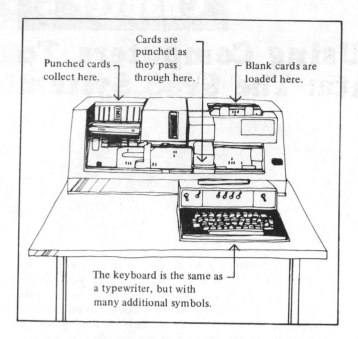

Figure 15. A keypunch machine

Figure 16. Loading a deck of cards into a *card reader*. The reader puts the information into the computer.

Although one can easily learn how to use a keypunch machine, it takes most people a long time to learn to keypunch with adequate speed and accuracy. This is because most data are numerical or contain many parentheses and punctuations which mean specific things to the computer. These must be typed with *100% accuracy*. The lack of a period or a space in any place on any card will make the computer unable to perform the analysis; the computer is totally unforgiving and makes little allowance for human error. You are strongly advised, consequently, to obtain the services of a keypunch operator.

In the interest of assessing accuracy, data should be *verified* after keypunching. To verify keypunching, the punched cards are fed through a machine like the keypunching machine while an operator retypes the whole set of data. If what is typed the second time is not the same as what was typed the first time, an error is detected. Because the verifying entails retyping the data set, it can be quite expensive.

A cheap alternative for small quantities of data is to make a *printout* of the cards on large computer paper and then check the printout visually. Cards can be printed out using a *list machine* which is usually available for use at no cost at the computer center. Of course *the cards themselves* can be checked for accuracy; but handling cards is cumbersome and if the edges become ragged, the *card reader*—the machine that reads the cards for the computer—may balk.

Entering Data Into the Computer

Knowing how data are entered into the computer will help you understand some of the details governing how it must be prepared. The discussion that follows takes a sample case—Jonathan Dough—and shows how information for Jonathan Dough is recorded on cards and is read into the computer along with other cases.

Recording data on cards

Suppose an experimental career education program has concluded its first year in several of a district's schools, with other schools serving as a control group. A *reading achievement test* is available for each student as an indicator of ability. In addition, each person's *English and math grades from last year* have been recorded. A *pretest* was administered at the beginning of the program to assess general knowledge about careers. During the program, *unit tests* were given regularly and scores assigned in the form of percent of items correct. Teachers supplied the data analyst with each student's *average score on these unit tests* and with a count of the *times the student was absent*. At the end of the program, *English and math grades over the school year* were again recorded, and the general career knowledge *posttest* was again administered.

For each student, such information has been punched on a card. Jonathan Dough's card is shown in Figure 17. An example of a corresponding *codebook page* is shown in Figure 18. Figure 18 should be studied along with Figure 17, since the codebook explains what each of the card's 80 columns means. The *codebook*, which is prepared by the data analyst, is constantly referred to during data analysis. If the codebook is complete and accurate, it will enable a data analyst who is not at all familiar with the data to analyze it when told what questions must be answered.

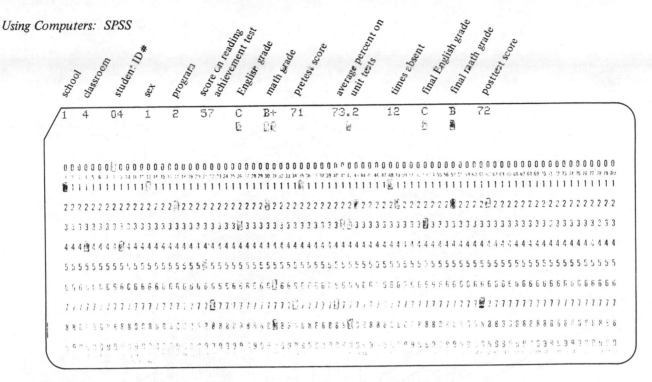

Figure 17. Jonathan Dough's data on a computer card. The computer reads the holes in the cards electronically. The printing along the top of the card is for the user to read, not the computer. Careful examination of this card and the codebook in Figure 18 tells you that Jonathan attends school 1 (Washington), is in classroom 4, has ID#04, is male, is in program 2 (experimental), and so forth. The card has 80 columns so a single card can carry a fair amount of data, especially since it is not necessary to leave spaces between the numbers or letters as has been done here. If there were so much information to be recorded that 80 columns were not sufficient, then one or more additional cards could be added for Jonathan directly behind the first one.

Column	Variable	Variable Name	Range of Values	Value Labels	Missing Value
1	school	SCHOOL	1-4	1=Washington 2=Jefferson 3=Reed 4=Kennedy	
4	classroom	CLASS	1-6	---	
8-9	student ID#	ID	1-50	---	
13	student sex	SEX	1-2	1=male 2=female	0
17	program	PROGRAM	1-3	1=experimental program A 2=experimental program B 3=control	
21-22	reading raw score on CTBA, Level 4, Form Q taken 9/20/76	READ	1-80	---	99

Figure 18. Sample codebook page. *Column* refers to the numbers of the 80 columns on the card. Each column can hold only one digit, letter, or symbol. Columns 8 and 9 are used to record a two-digit student ID#: Jonathan's ID# is 04. *Variable* and *variable name* are short names given to each piece of information for use in the computer. In the SPSS system, the variable name must not be more than eight characters long. Choosing a name that is a mnemonic for the variable is helpful for the user. *Range of values* lists the symbols the computer can expect to receive designating categories to which different variables might be assigned. For example, since there are three programs, the program variable might take on the value 1, 2, or 3. *Missing value* indicates symbols that the user has chosen to enter for missing data. For example, the reading score is recorded as 99 if no score is available for a student. If the columns were left blank, the reading score might be read as zero. The value chosen for a missing value must be, of course, outside the *range of values* for the variable.

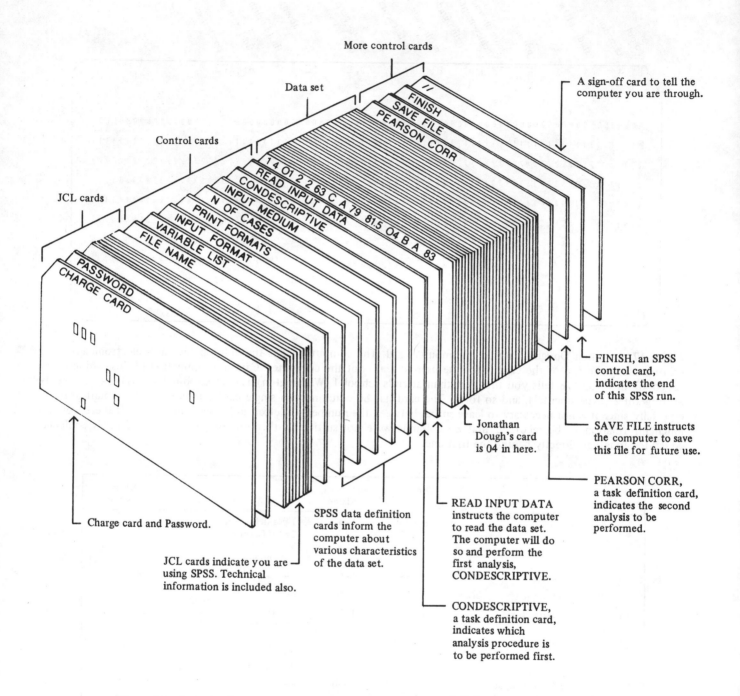

Figure 19. A deck of computer cards ready for entry. Cards are read from front to back.

Preparing a deck of cards for reading by the computer

When cards like the one in Figure 17 have been punched to record the data from all participating students, the *data set,* one portion of the *deck* of cards which will be submitted to the computer, is complete. Now the *computer* has to be told how to *find* information on the cards, and it has to receive directions about what computations and analyses to perform. The cards that give these directions to the com-

puter are called *SPSS control cards.* The control cards, plus a few cards that tell the computer to run SPSS and charge the job to you, must be added to the data set to complete the deck. Figure 19 shows the card deck for the career education program example. Note that most of the control cards *precede* the data set in the deck. Though the SPSS manual explains the control cards in detail, a few of them are described here to illustrate what they do.

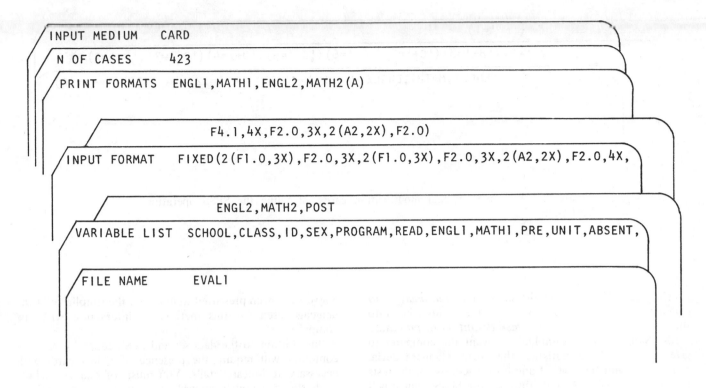

Figure 20. Examples of data definition SPSS control cards for the career education example deck in Figure 19

SPSS control cards are of two types: *data definition* cards which tell the computer about the data set and how to read it, and *task definition* cards, which tell the computer which analyses to perform. First the data definition cards:

1. One of the control cards gives the computer a name for the data set you are entering for each particular run. This name is called the *file name,* and it must be no longer than eight adjacent characters. Putting data into the computer is like putting it into a filing cabinet; the file of data should be given a name so that it can be found again in the future. If you were conducting several evaluation studies, you might name the data sets from each study by different names or call them something like EVAL1, EVAL2, and so forth. Any particular set of data that you wish to keep separate can be labeled by means of a card like the one at the front of the control cards in Figure 20. This card establishes a file name EVAL1 for the careers program evaluation, EVALU-ATION STUDY #1.

2. Another control card lists the *variables* that the computer will read. For the data set to which Jonathan Dough belongs, the variable list has been determined by the codebook shown in Figure 18. The variable card tells the computer the names assigned to the card columns used in the data set. The user is free to name variables anything he wishes as long as names do not exceed eight characters in length. The 14 variable names on the vari-

able list card in Figure 20 identify the 14 pieces of information that the data analyst entered for each student.

3. A control card called the *input format* card tells the computer in which columns of each card to find each variable.

4. The *print formats* card is an optional control card used only when some of the data are alphabetical rather than numerical, such as the English and math scores on Jonathan Dough's card. *Print formats* tells the computer which data entries will be non-numbers.

5. Another card, *N of cases,* informs the computer how many cases there are in the data set.

6. The *input medium card* tells the computer whether the data set is on cards, disc, or tape.

7. Another kind of control card which does not appear in the deck in Figure 19 is the *data modification card.* This card is used to *change* the data in some way. For example, if grades have been recorded as letters and you wish to calculate average grades, it will be necessary to change the letters to numbers. This is easily accomplished by a procedure called RECODE. For example, to recode English and math scores in Jonathan Dough's data, you would enter cards like those in Figure 21 among the control cards.

Instructions for preparation of these and other control cards are in the **SPSS** manual.

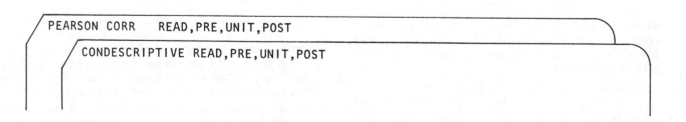

```
                    ('F '=1)
          ('B '=9)('B-'=8)('C+'=7)('C '=6)('C-'=5)('D+'=4)('D '=3)('D-'=2)
  RECODE       ENGL1,MATH1,ENGL2,MATH2('A+'=13)('A '=12)('A-'=11)('B+'=10)
```

Figure 21. Example of data modification cards signaling the SPSS operation RECODE

The user must also tell the computer *what analyses to perform* with the data set. This is done by inserting, into the deck, control cards called *task definition* or *procedure* cards. Suppose, for example, you want the computer to give you descriptive statistics—the mean, standard deviation, range, and the highest and lowest scores—for the tests in the variable list. A look through the SPSS manual will show that these statistics can all be obtained by using the single code word CONDESCRIPTIVE and listing the variables for which you require these statistics. Thus you might prepare a card like the front card in Figure 22.

When SPSS is used with cards, the first analysis to be performed is inserted into the deck behind the last data definition card. It is followed by a card marked READ INPUT DATA, and then the data set. If you wanted additional analyses, for example *correlations* between test scores, you would enter a card marked, for instance, PEARSON CORR naming the particular correlation coefficient you want the computer to compute and the variables to be correlated. Such a card appears in Figure 22. Other cards naming additional analyses would follow.

The SPSS manual gives directions for preparing both the data definition and task definition cards. The few examples

above have been presented to illustrate the simplicity of the language used for this method of interaction with the computer.

In addition to the data set and SPSS control cards, the computer will require the presence of a few cards with necessary technical details. You must, of course, include cards showing your password and charge account number. You will also attach some technical language cards called *Job Control Language* or JCL cards. One of these informs the computer that you wish to use the SPSS system. Other JCL cards determine how much time and space the computer must set aside for you. You must get help from the professional staff at the computer center to prepare JCL cards. Whereas the SPSS control cards can be easily figured out from the manual, JCL cards vary from one computer center to another and are best requested from center personnel.

If a SAVE FILE control card has been inserted at the rear of the deck, as in Figure 19, the computer will *save* the data and the data-defining information as a *file*, named according to the instructions on your FILE NAME card. This eliminates the trouble of resubmitting all the data when you want to run additional analyses. For these subse-

```
  PEARSON CORR    READ,PRE,UNIT,POST
    CONDESCRIPTIVE READ,PRE,UNIT,POST
```

Figure 22. Examples of task definition SPSS control cards. Their placement in the deck is illustrated in Figure 19.

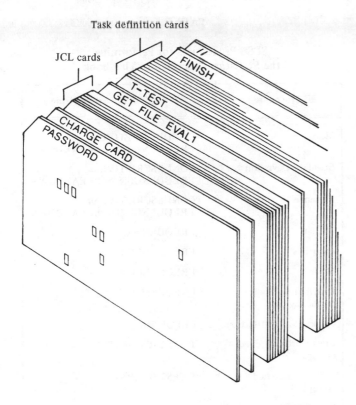

Task definition cards

JCL cards

FINISH

T-TEST

GET FILE EVAL1

CHARGE CARD

PASSWORD

Figure 23. Computer cards ready for entry to run a program for which data are already on file

quent runs, you can enter a much smaller deck that looks like Figure 23. A GET FILE card retrieves all the data definition information and the data set by referencing the file name you gave in the first run.

Preparing Data for Computer Analysis

The information in this section is important whether you plan to do the computer work yourself or hire an assistant. Either way, *it is essential that you establish an accurate system for collecting and recording data.*

The management of data is not usually a simple matter; numerous problems can arise. Getting all the right information onto the proper cards and into the proper files demands careful data collection and organization *before* anyone sits down to keypunch. *The best defense against data management problems is advance planning and installation of a workable system.* Such a system should be devised by the person who will analyze the data in consultation with the data gatherers—teachers, observers, whomever—involved. The system must somehow get the data from its point of origin (for instance, a student test, an observation schedule or questionnaire, a set of school records) onto the computer card without error or loss.

The most essential component of a data management plan is a *master list* of cases (usually people) which includes

ID numbers. The purpose of the master list is to ensure that scores on each measure are attributed to the right person. You should begin the master list by arranging in order the names of, say, the students from whom you first collected data. By the end of data collection, the list should include the names of *everyone* from whom *any* data was obtained, even if his data are incomplete. The master list keeps track of everyone. Each name should be assigned an identification number; and in situations where confidentiality is important, names corresponding to the ID numbers should be kept in a separate file. ID numbers, once assigned, should never be changed.

Once the list has been written down, *no changes should be made* in the order of the names. *If a student drops out,* the name should nevertheless remain on the list to prevent confusion of that person's data with someone else's. Data set cards for dropouts should even be keypunched using a symbol from the codebook that signals to the computer that data are missing.

If students join the program, their names should be added at the end of the list, and new ID numbers assigned. To allow this and still keep track of students, compose ID numbers that classify students according to, say, school and classroom, rather than relying on a strictly numerical order. In this way, student number 04 in one class can be distinguished from student number 04 in another by combining the 04 with his school and class number. Thus 1104 is student 04 from class 1 in school 1 while 3204 is student 04 from class 2 in school 3. New students are added to the SPSS data file by using a control card called ADD CASES.

```
School ID# 3                          Class ID# 2

ID#        Student          Pretest   Posttest

01      Apple, Arlene          10        30
02      Benny, Brian           07        99  ←
03      Cooper, Carol          08        32
04      Dixon, David           05        99  ←
05      Evans, Earl            13        43

06      Mann, Marlene          12        40
07      Sanchez, Saul          13        38
08      Venn, Valerie          09        33
09      Zee, Zelda             08        35
10      Newcomer, Norman       99  ←      31
11      Arroyo, Arturo         99  ←      32
```

These students entered late. Their names are added at the end of the list, not squeezed in alphabetically.

These students missed the pretest or posttest. A code indicates that data are missing.

Figure 24. Portion of a master list for data management

It is not necessary to wait for posttest data before setting up the SPSS data file; in fact it is wise to set it up right after the pretest rather than wait until the rush that follows posttesting. Once a file has been saved on the SPSS system, new information such as posttest scores can be added by means of a control card called ADD VARI- ABLES. This procedure can only be used if there is an exact match between the number of cases in the file and the number of cases for whom new information is to be added. This is another reason why *no changes must be made in the master list*.

Some Statistical Analyses That Can Be Performed Using SPSS

SPSS provides a variety of tests and analyses. Table 5 matches the statistical procedures presented in this book with SPSS procedures that accomplish the same tasks by computer.

Besides these, you might want to use one or more of the many more complex analyses that SPSS makes possible. This section briefly describes the most common statistical analyses performed by computer.

Analysis of variance (SPSS procedure name: ANOVA). Perhaps the most important procedure not included here but available on SPSS is analysis of variance. While the t-test, discussed in Chapter 3, provides a way of checking the statistical significance of the difference between mean scores from *two* groups, analysis of variance can examine differences among *three or more means*. The SPSS procedure called ONEWAY is excellent for contrasting three or more programs on a single outcome measure.

Partial correlation (SPSS procedure name: PARTIAL CORR). A partial correlation coefficient shows the correlation between two measures when a third factor thought to influence the correlation is "controlled for." Suppose, for example, that you want to know the correlation between regularity of attendance and program achievement: a high correlation would indicate that higher attendance levels are associated with higher achievement, a finding that would suggest an effective program. However, since *ability* strongly influences achievement, you might want to perform a correlation which removes, in essence, the effects of ability. You would use PARTIAL CORR in SPSS to compute the partial correlation between posttest and atten- dance with ability controlled for.

Analysis of covariance (An optional procedure available along with ANOVA, analysis of variance). Analysis of covariance is conceptually similar to partial correlation. It is used to control for factors influencing an *analysis of vari- ance* rather than a correlation, however. Analysis of covari- ance is sometimes viewed as a way to make interpretable the results from a pretest-posttest control group study which shows an unfortunate result: *pretest* scores of the experimental and control groups are different. To permit conclusions to be made from the *posttest* scores, pretest scores should be the same. Analysis of covariance can statistically adjust posttest scores to remove the effects of this initial difference. Unfortunately, the procedure may under- or overcorrect, and its use involves assumptions

TABLE 5

SPSS Procedures for Performing the Statistics Described in This Book

Procedure	SPSS Procedure Name
Mean	CONDESCRIPTIVE or FREQUENCIES or BREAKDOWN
Standard Deviation	CONDESCRIPTIVE or FREQUENCIES or BREAKDOWN
Variance	CONDESCRIPTIVE or FREQUENCIES or BREAKDOWN
Median	FREQUENCIES
Quartiles	FREQUENCIES
Mode	FREQUENCIES
Distribution (score-frequency list)	FREQUENCIES
Graph of a Distribution	FREQUENCIES
t-test for Unmatched Groups	T-TEST (GROUPS)
t-test for Matched Groups	T-TEST (PAIRS)
Plot of Two Sets of Data (a correlaion graph)	SCATTERGRAM
Phi Coefficient	CROSSTABS
Point Biserial r	PEARSON CORR or CROSSTABS or SCATTERGRAM
Pearson's Product Moment Correlation Coefficient	PEARSON CORR or CROSSTABS or SCATTERGRAM
Spearman's Rank Order Correlation Coefficient	NONPAR CORR
Chi-square	CROSSTABS
Contingency Table	CROSSTABS

about various features of the data that frequently cannot be met. *Most* statistical tests are, of course, based on assump- tions; but violation of these alters their accuracy very little. Analysis of covariance is an exception and may mislead you considerably if improperly used.[18]

Multiple regression (SPSS procedure name: REGRES- SION). Simple regression is just the correlation of *two* variables, as described in Chapter 4. Multiple regression correlates one characteristic with a *set* of others. For ex- ample, you might want to know whether achievement on a math test is related to IQ, socio-economic status, length of experience of the math teacher, *and* attitude about math. Given scores on tests of all these variables from a sample of

18. Elashoff, J. D. Analysis of covariance: A delicate instru- ment. *American Educational Research Journal*, 1969, 6(3), 383-401.

students, the REGRESSION procedure can set up an equation showing the extent to which math achievement can be predicted from the other characteristics. Regression equations should be interpreted with great caution and employed only with large samples, say 60 or more cases. If many variables are used, ability to predict a certain outcome might look spuriously strong. Before much confidence is placed in a regression equation, it should be checked by administering the measures to another sample of students. Or, if the original sample is sufficiently large—more than 100—you could divide it randomly in half and treat your work as two multiple regression studies which cross-check each other.

Discriminant analysis (SPSS procedure name: DISCRIMINANT). Discriminant analysis identifies factors that distinguish Group A from Group B or from Group C. For example, participants in a program might be classified as *satisfied* with it, or *displeased,* on the basis of a questionnaire item. Other questionnaire items, and results from other measures such as achievement or age, could be examined to look for variables which distinguish people who are pleased with the program from those who are displeased.

Factor analysis (SPSS procedure name: FACTOR). If you have a large number of measures, say 10 or more, administered to a large number of cases, at least 100, *and* you wonder if there might be some way to grasp the data and interpret the scores in terms of a *few simple factors,* then you may wish to run a factor analysis. Factor analysis is a procedure that starts out by correlating every variable with every other variable. These inter-correlations are then examined to find patterns. Factor analysis is a complex procedure and should be done by an expert.

These more complex procedures demand a level of statistical expertise beyond most novices. A well-trained data analyst can tell you not only how to perform these analyses, but can alert you to cases in which the complex procedures might create more confusion than understanding in your situation.

Index